# HOME TOWN

by

## SHERWOOD ANDERSON

PHOTOGRAPHS BY FARM SECURITY PHOTOGRAPHERS

*With an Introduction by*
DAVID D. ANDERSON

PAUL P. APPEL, PUBLISHER
MAMARONECK, NEW YORK
1975

Library of Congress Catalog Card Number: 75-10684

# INTRODUCTION

by

David D. Anderson

When Sherwood Anderson published *Home Town* in 1940, he was nearly at the end of his long creative career; the only work he was yet to write was some of that incorporated in his *Memoirs,* unfinished at his death. Thus, for all practical purposes *Home Town* stands as Anderson's final statement of what he had found meaningful in a life marked by the rejection of many of the values of his time and the reaffirmation of others.

Two versions of *Home Town* exist, that in this volume and a somewhat longer version, published as "The American Small Town" in *The Sherwood Anderson Reader,* edited by Anderson's friend Paul Rosenfeld. Differences exist that are technical and detailed rather than substantive, but both versions are alike in their insistence upon the closeness of the relationship between Anderson and the reality as well as the ideal of the small town, as he celebrates both. In the prefatory statement of the longer version, Anderson makes clear the nature of the small-town man as he has known it:

> Perhaps only a passionate traveler like myself can realize how lucky he is to be able to call a small town his home. My work is constantly calling me away from Marion, but I always hunger to get back. There is in the life

of the small town a possibility of intimacy, a chance to know others—an intimacy oftentimes frightening, but which can be healing. Day after day, under all sorts of circumstances, in sickness and health, in good fortune and bad, we small-towners are close to one another and know each other in ways the city man can never experience. A man goes away and comes back. Certain people have died. Babies have been born. Children of yesterday have suddenly become young men and women. Life has been going on. Still nothing has really changed. On the streets, day after day, mostly the same faces. There is this narrow but fascinating panorama. In a way it is too intimate. Life can never be intimate enough.

Anderson has described the passage of time and the essential timelessness of the small town elsewhere in more detail, but here, in these few words and in the long essay that *Home Town* essentially is, he has described it more eloquently and with more deeply-felt emotion than ever before.

However, neither the eloquent definition nor the deep feeling had come easy for Anderson, who, nearly forty-five years before, had been one of countless young men from Midwestern small towns who sought their fortunes and their fulfillment in the metropolis of Chicago. With an insight that carries with it the power of poetry and the depth of myth he described that departure symbolically if not factually at the end of *Winesburg, Ohio,* when he wrote:

The young man's mind was carried away by his growing passion for dreams. One looking at him would not have thought him particularly sharp. With the recollection of little things occupying his mind he closed his eyes and leaned back in the car seat. He stayed that way for a long time and when he aroused himself and again looked out of the car window the town of Winesburg had disappeared and his life there had become but a background on which to point the dreams of his manhood.

The finality of this fictional departure was no less so than Anderson's departure from Clyde, Ohio, for Chicago in the Fall of 1896, returning only briefly to leave for the Spanish-American War with the local infantry company in 1898, and then to be mustered out a year later. Anderson's break with Clyde and with what it represented was to him permanent; the success that he sought could be found only in a city, and nearly thirty years was to pass until, his life and his career gone nearly full circle, he found acceptance and closeness in Marion, Virginia.

The history of that circle is too long to recount here, but in essence it is in microcosm the search for permanence and values that has marked the course of the twentieth century for many Americans, perhaps even for the country itself. When Anderson, like his fictional counterpart George Willard, left the small town behind, he was also leaving behind America's nineteenth-century past, a past compounded largely of hardship and innocence. His path paralleled those of Theodore Dreiser, from Terre Haute, Indiana, Carl Sandburg from Galesburg, Illinois, Edgar Lee Masters from Lewistown, Illinois, and a variety of others, all of whom, without knowing they were doing so, were following paths laid out a decade or more earlier by George Ade, Opie Read, Ben King, Finley Peter Dunne, and others. Post-Civil War, post-fire Chicago was not only "Hog butcher to the world" and center of the mail-order business, but it was also a modest cultural and literary center.

Anderson's path to literary greatness and ultimately back to his symbolic origins was neither direct nor easy; it was marked by an apprenticeship in advertising writing, a brief stint as president of a mail-order firm, and a longer period as president of his own mail-order paint company. Finally it was marked by a rejection of commercial values that, transmuted into myth, was to become the point of departure for his writing career, the subject of much of his early fiction, a constant souce of wonder to himself, and the point at which he began his long symbolic and literal search for his beginnings.

As he moved toward literary greatness and ultimately toward the affirmative statement in *Home Town,* Anderson left behind him numerous literary landmarks, among them some of the most significant and influential works in modern American literary history. His first two novels, *Windy McPherson's Son* (1916) and *Marching Men* (1917), both of them remnants of the secret writing he had done in Elyria, Ohio, were powerful statements of rejection—rejection of the materialistic promises of modern business and industrialism, promises that had been propagated in his youth hundreds of times by Horatio Alger Jr., Russell Conwell, and countless others—and of affirmation of the human values by which man might give meaning and direction to his life. But both novels are flawed by the ambiguity with which Anderson attempted to define those human values. Convinced that they existed and that they were attainable by those who had rejected the new American industrial society, nevertheless he had no idea of where or how they might be found.

However, Anderson followed these first two novels with a volume dominated by unabashed celebration, *Mid-American Chants* (1918). Anderson's first volume of poetry, *Mid-American Chants* is not only Anderson's attempt to fulfill the letter of his contract for three books with his publisher, as some critics have dismissed it; it is a work that celebrates rejection, both symbolic and literal, and that proclaims his faith in the durability of the Midwestern countryside and the human spirit. The product of the years that saw *Winesburg, Ohio* (1918) become a reality, not only does it proclaim a faith without the ambiguity of his earlier novels, but it is tangible evidence of the direction in which his search for permanence and meaning was taking him.

At the same time this volume of verse, for all its naivete, points out the direction that Anderson's future work was to take, particularly in his next two publications, both of them new, both original, both major works in his career and in the literature of his time. These were *Winesburg, Ohio* and *Poor White* (1921).

The collection of short stories and sketches that is *Winesburg, Ohio* is the product of the same years in which Anderson celebrated his origins and his faith in the *Chants,* but it is not a work of celebration; rather, it is a work of exploration, a work whose logical culmination is the affirmation of *Home Town* a generation later. Anderson's most substantial and justly celebrated work, *Winesburg, Ohio* is a return to origins, not only in his boyhood home of Clyde, Ohio, but also in the boarding house of his early years of return to Chicago. Both places were curiously alike, both microcosms of human experience, and in both he found it possible to examine closely those whose spirits had been deformed by confused values, not only those of material fulfillment but also of the dehumanized spiritual denial of the necessity of human love.

But at this time Anderson was still convinced that the people of Winesburg were buried in the past of America's innocence, an innocence impossible to resurrect in the twentieth century, and in *Poor White* he determined to explore the process by which values had become distorted and people twisted as the past of their innocence was destroyed. *Poor White* is not indignant, as were Anderson's early novels; instead it explores the promise, the potential, and the failure of modern American technology. Anderson taps the roots of human experience in America: the preoccupation with movement; the mystic memory of the river and its rejection; the rise of the railroads and the attempt to replace drudgery with leisure; the images of Abraham Lincoln and Mark Twain as they contributed to and were absorbed by the growing myth of America; the rise and fall of craftsmanship and of simple human pride.

Again in *Poor White* Anderson symbolically rejected the new America, as his central character began his search for closeness and love in a new, uncomplicated relationship with his wife. Again, however, Anderson's uncertainty flaws the novel as he ends on a note of ambiguity. Clearly, Anderson knew that human values and industrial domination were incompatible, but he still had no idea whether or not a spiritual reality might overcome and replace values manufactured by machinery.

With the publication of *Poor White* Anderson had completed the philosophical foundations of *Home Town,* but he had yet to re-identify its reality in twentieth century America. The fame and notoriety of a prominent literary career began to affect him adversely—praise was phony and denunciation was demoralizing—and he began tentatively to break the ties that he had made in the literary world, just as he had broken those that had held him to business. In the 1920's he alternately wandered America, to New York, to Reno, to California, to New Orleans, to the rural South, and he wrote—two volumes of stories, many of them major, and a weak and repetitious but symbolically important novel, *Many Marriages* (1923). "How many marriages among people!" Anderson cried out as he sought meaningful relationships after the fact of rejection, and he did so again in *Dark Laughter* (1925), another story of rejection and search. Close to a best-seller, *Dark Laughter* is unfortunately underestimated by many critics as it returns in subject matter to the tap roots of Anderson's and America's youth: the river, the small town, the craftsman's bench, the innocent, simple people who are intuitively wise, the wandering sophisticate, convinced that ". . . he, in common with almost all American men, had got out of touch with things—stones lying in fields, the fields themselves, houses, trees, rivers, factory walls, tools, women's bodies . . ." Again Anderson ended on a note of ambiguity, however, as fulfillment seemed just beyond reach.

During these years of wandering Anderson turned, too, to autobiography, to the attempt to re-explore and re-interpret the facts of his origins, his family, his experience, and, alternately affirming and despairing, he reiterated the values he had found permanent and fulfilling: the touch of a mother's hand, the pride inherent in craftsmanship, an understanding of his father as he exorcised the ghost of Windy McPherson; a conviction, in spite of the evidence, that human closeness is not impossible or absurd. In these autobiographies, *A Story Teller's Story* (1924), *Sherwood Anderson's Notebook* (1926), and *Tar: A Midwest Childhood* (1926), Anderson admitted that he was not concerned with facts but with feelings as he attempted to define not only values but a way of life that was possible only after the rejection of material values and the affirmation of human honesty, sincerity, closeness, and love.

In essence these values are those defined in terms of human experience in *Home Town,* but for Anderson they were values ignored or denied by the America of which he had been part for almost all of his adult life—the America of Chicago, Cleveland, and Elyria; of cold-storage warehouses, advertising offices, and sales rooms; of the army of late nineteenth century imperialism; of sophisticated literary and artistic circles who had declared that their "revolt from the village" had been successful and permanent. The values of this phase of Anderson's life were those of his and America's innocence and childhood; the products of the past, these values, Anderson believed, had no reality except in his memory, his feeling, even his nostalgic recreation of the past.

Nevertheless, just as this introspection permitted Anderson to re-define those values, his wandering taught him that they still existed in an America as yet untouched by either materialism or sophistication: in the hills of Western Virginia, where in 1925, he established himself at Ripshin Farm near Troutdale and two years later purchased and edited two weekly newspapers, *The Smyth County News,* Republican, and the *Marion Democrat,* Democratic, in nearby Marion. From the mid-1920's to the end of his life fifteen years later, he maintained a close personal relationship with the farm, the papers, and the town.

During these last years Anderson was neither a recluse nor a refugee from the twentieth century. Neither did he live an idyllic life remote from central experience of his time, nor did he condescend to become a local celebrity. Rather, he entered into the life of the town as an editor, he developed a social consciousness and political awareness virtually non-existent in his earlier works, he published fifteen more books, including some of his best work, and he entered into his fourth, most durable and satisfying marriage. During these years he also traveled widely, returning to his home in the hills after each venture abroad. In spite of periods of disillusionment and despair, these were certainly the happiest, most fulfilling years of his life.

The record of Anderson's literary accomplishment during those years is substantial, it represents some considerable departures from his past work, and it makes clear the new commitment to old values that his discovery of the Virginia hill country had made possible for him. His re-discovery of humanized reality is celebrated in his second volume of verse, *A New Testament* (1927); in two novels *Beyond Desire* (1932) and *Kit Brandon* (1936), the former an exploration of the uncertainties, the confused loyalties, and the bewilderment inherent in the search for meaning and identity in the labor strife of the Southern mill towns, and the latter, the rise of the new, free woman who exploits the machine and the weaknesses of men as she finds her own human identity. A short volume of short stories, *Death in the Woods* (1933), contains some of his best short fiction, including both the title story and "Brother Death," written as a capstone for the volume. *Hello Towns!* (1929), the result of his venture into journalism, directly anticipates *Home Town* as it draws on the columns of his papers for its substance and emulates the cycle of time and of human life in its structure. Indicative of what journalism can be at its best, it was followed by the journalistic record of ventures into the world in *Perhaps Women* (1931), *No Swank* (1934), and *Puzzled America* (1935), all of them indicative of his concern with the growing potential of women, the permanence of human relations, and the economic failure and human triumph of the Depression.

In a series of short, limited works, *Nearer the Grass Roots* (1929), *Alice and the Lost Novel* (1929), and the *American County Fair* (1930), he began his affirmation of human durability, and in the last years of his life, perhaps recognizing that his life had indeed emulated the natural cycle with which he had become concerned, he began work on his *Memoirs,* incomplete at his death and published in edited versions in 1942 and in 1969. During his last year he completed the manuscript of *Home Town.*

Of all the range of Anderson's work, none is more suitable as a final statement of his understanding of life than *Home Town.* In its profundity it is simple as it indicates that he had indeed re-discovered what he had left behind him years before in Clyde, Ohio, when he went off to Chicago to seek his fortune or, in *Poor White,* when Bidwell, Ohio, became a major industrial city.

During his last years, as Hitler moved into Austria, Czechoslovakia, and Poland, as Depression lessened while America moved closer to participation in war in Europe and Asia, Anderson wrote in the room he called his "Rogue's Gallery," lined with photographs of friends out of his past, and in his writing he evoked the permanence he found possible in intimate human relations. *Home Town* is an eloquent testimony to the depth of feeling that he explored.

*Home Town* is Anderson's tribute to the source of all that he had found meaningful in his long creative career, and it is his final definition of the values which America might use as the foundation for a new, humanized post-Depression society. Not only a tribute to America's past, it is at the same time a testimony to his hope for the future.

At the heart of Anderson's faith is an acceptance of nature itself, the foundation and the wellspring from which all human life comes. The small town, "...halfway between the cities whence we get the ideas and the soil whence we get the strength," is America in microcosm and in reality, and, Anderson asserts, to be a townsman is to live in harmony with both nature and the nation.

Thus *Home Town* uses as its foundation the cycle of nature that activates and directs the life of the town at the same time that it makes possible the intimacies of its life. Spring is the time when life quickens, trees bloom, grass grows green, and the town ball team begins to practice and to seek financial support. While the kids start to think about fields and creeks and the town iconoclast has his annual bath and shave, the pace of life quickens as blood and sap run faster.

Spring becomes summer, a time of growth, of restlessness, and of hard work that leads to harvest and fulfillment. During the long days and evenings, while parents look on, kids learn about life and about nature, sometimes to the town's disapproval. "Hot, dusty days, long days, summer rains — the summer days are the best of all the year's days for the American small-towner," Anderson writes, as summer becomes fall, "... the checking-up time, the harvesting of the year's efforts of the American man to survive, getting a little forward in life." Winter approaches, evocative of nostalgia, fear, and promise as the cycle moves on, always the same and yet different.

Upon this framework of the natural cycle, Anderson constructs in microcosm the essence of American life, a kaleidoscopic montage of the town's people. The gossip, the politician, the chicken thief, the boy whose nerve fails him as he approaches the small house on the back street, the moralist, the merchant, the editor, all mingle on the main street, in the churches, the schools, and new ideas filter in to adapt subtly to change, as the larger world beyond threatens the life of the town.

In spite of the threats sensed from without, Anderson suggests that the town and its values are permanent and immutable. As the seasons change, the town reflects in turn nature's hope, its fulfillment, its need. And in the midst of that natural cycle Anderson makes clear the search for the intimacy that makes human life possible and worthwhile. Man is his brother's keeper, Anderson proclaims, but only in the towns is he willing to accept that responsibility, a responsibility that makes human life endurable.

Not only has Anderson written his most deeply-felt prose in this essay, but he has also done some of his best writing. His prose is smooth and rhythmical as it reflects the essence of American speech. His vignettes of life are sharply etched, and they are true, as Anderson had always insisted upon truth in his work. "It must be that I am an incurable small town man," he had confessed a year earlier in a talk at Olivet College in Michigan, and in *Home Town* he makes clear what he had learned in leaving and in rediscovering the American town. In the process he makes clear the ultimate value of life in all of America as he had known it.

Anderson's vision and prose provide the substance of this volume, but the included photographs give it a depth and a presence impossible for words alone. The product of the decade that produced the photo essay, photo journalism, and the photo record, the selected pictures are the work of men and women whose names are synonymous with photography at its mature best. Under the sponsorship of the Farm Security Administration, one of the New Deal's many attempts to overcome the Depression, and coordinated by Roy E. Stryker, photographers — Ben Shahn, Walker Evans, Arthur Rothstein, Marion Post, Dorothea Lange, and dozens of others — roamed rural America, just as Sherwood Anderson had done for much of his life. The photographers attempted to record photographically and permanently a nation in flux, a way of life threatened by the forces of change, and yet, in the simple dignity of its people, a nation firmly rooted in the American tradition. Anderson's prose and these first-rate photographs combine to provide a statement about the nature of America that endures in spite of changing fashions, restless movement, scandal, or war. Technology, Anderson concludes and these photographs reiterate, can only provide a further dimension of life and nature to the people, those who are the essence of the towns and of America as well.

Lansing, Michigan David D. Anderson
February, 1974

# LIST OF PHOTOGRAPHERS AND PICTURE LOCATIONS

# HOME TOWN

## I

THERE IS A LONG LETTER on my desk from a young man. Something I have written and that has been published has upset him. He is one of the young men you meet everywhere now. He has a burning desire to remake life, the whole social scheme. He is a little fretful and angry at me because I like the Oak Hills, the smaller scenes, because I have doubts about the ends to be achieved by trying to be a big thinker, a mover of masses of men.

He scolds at me. I had somewhere said something about the necessity nowadays of staying put. In saying that, I had in mind staying closer home in our thoughts and feelings. The big world outside now is so filled with confusion. It seemed to me that our only hope, in the present muddle, was to try thinking small.

It must be that the young man who has written the letter to me feels that he has something great to give to the world. In his letter he speaks of the rapidity with which men now move from place to place. I had, in what I had written, spoken about the advisability of a man's wanting to live fully, at the beginning, in a small way; trying, for example, to get a little better understanding of the people in his own house, in the street on which his house stands; trying to get closer to the people of his own town.

It had seemed to me, as I wrote, that a man like Lincoln must have begun like that. With what strange sadness he left the then small town of Springfield, Illinois, to become President. There was a little speech made to the people of the town at the railroad station when he left, and it is one of the most moving things in literature. As you read, you feel Lincoln was a man who grew like a tree, beginning small, getting keen understanding of the little life about him and emerging into the large.

The young man who has written to me says that he is going off to New York City. He feels that he must get among other intellectuals, bigger people than he finds in his home town, people who have bigger thoughts, vaster dreams. He declares that the day of the individual has passed, that now we must think of people only in the mass. A man must learn to love and work for the masses.

The proletariat, the middle class, the capitalist class! A man is no longer just a man going along, trying a little to cultivate his own senses, trying to see more, hear more. That day has passed now. The young man feels that Oak Hill is not big enough for the big life he says he feels in himself. It may be that I am being unfair to him. It seems to me that a man like Lincoln would still have been Lincoln had he never left Springfield, Illinois; that he grew naturally, as a tree grows, out of the soil of Springfield, Illinois, out of the people about him whom he knew so intimately.

It seems to me that he grew out of a house, a street, a shabby little country lawyer's office; out of his touch with the common men he met in little country courtrooms; and that all this made him the man he became.

It may be that there is a bigness every man should seek, but the world is full now of false bigness, men speaking at meetings, trying to move masses of other men, getting a big feeling in that way; there's a trickiness in that approach to others—through applause, feeling a false power and importance.

**The people he knew so intimately...**

The Oak Hills are too small for such men. Their own houses are too small. They must have a great field, millions of men as listeners to their voices.

The young man who wrote is half-angry with me because I said to him, "Why not Oak Hill? What's the matter with Oak Hill?"

He can't wait for the slow growth of understanding of others in such a small place. That is what he says.

He says that he is going to New York and that in the great city he will learn to give himself to others.

He declares he can't do it in Oak Hill, that he isn't understood there. He feels cramped.

But as I read his letter I kept asking myself over and over the same question:

"What's the matter with Oak Hill?"

I kept remembering that when Lincoln left Springfield, he asked his partner in a country law office to leave his name on the sign hanging out of the office window. He dreamed of coming back and taking up his old life in a small circle.

It must have been his ability to move and feel and live within the small scene that made him so effective in the larger place and that has left him such a vivid figure in our minds.

All of the big world outside was just more and more Springfields to him.

What's the matter with Oak Hill?

Why not Oak Hill?

...because I like
the smaller scenes...

## II

Do YOU REMEMBER WHEN YOU, now for so long a city man, your hair graying, were a small town boy and what the railroad meant to you? Did you dream of some day being a railroad engineer? Now the new streamline trains go whirling through the towns at eighty, ninety, a hundred miles an hour. There is the soft purr of a mail plane far overhead, cars from many states go dashing through.

All over America, in the towns, we speak the English language but the stream of English blood in us grows thinner and thinner. It has been growing thinner ever since the Revolutionary War.

Gradually a new pattern is being woven. The American, mixture of many bloods, grows constantly into a definite new race. It is a race that can be studied, understood best in the towns.

In the cities the new people, as they came in, tended to group themselves. There was an Italian section, the German, Chinese, a section filled with men from Southeastern Europe.

In the small towns this couldn't happen. Men went out along the railroads, settled in the towns, became a part of the town life. The new America was being made there. It is still being made.

With the coming of the railroads there was a new influx of strange people. England no longer sent its emigrants here. They went out to England's own colonies. The great Irish emigration began, the Germans came in hundreds of thousands, the Danes, the Swedes, the Norsemen, the Finns came.

It was the great period of building, of town making, the men of Northern Europe pushing up into Wisconsin, Minnesota, the great Northwest, to become lumbermen there, new farmers and town workmen, makers of more towns.

Then the Italians, Greeks, men of all Southwest Europe. Mexicans came up into the Southwest, the Asiatics into the Pacific coast country. The sons and daughters of all these learning to speak English, helping us in the making of a new language, the American language.

New life. New dreams in the heads of the boys of the towns.

But now the flow of new blood is stopping. There is a checking up, a grouping in new worlds of thought and feeling, government no longer a thing far off, touching but lightly small town life, a radio in almost every man's house now, the President speaking, Walter Winchell, a Hillbilly band, a famous singer.

The market place come into the sitting rooms of small frame houses in the towns, tooth paste, hair restorers, trade with South America, fascism, communism, the Yanks have beaten the White Sox, the old quiet sleepiness at evenings in the towns quite gone.

Still babies being born, lads with their lassies in cars parked under trees, hopes and dreams, the life in the towns still more leisurely, the same faces on the streets day after day, the problem of living with others a little closer, more persistently present. The real test of democracy may come in the towns.

San Augustine, Texas

**Moundville, Alabama**

Lancaster, Ohio

The real test of democracy...

...may come in the towns

## III

THE BOY LEAVES HIS HOME TOWN to go away to some city and his name is mentioned in his small town paper.

"Ed Horner has gone to Chicago (or it may be New York or Cleveland or Boston or St. Louis). He is about to accept a lucrative position in the city."

It is very strange. If we take the local editor's word for it all the small town boys get lucrative positions.

Such a young man may spend the greater part of his life in the city, but all his life he will remember the first day or night of his arrival in the city, the strange fear of the vast crowds of people pressing in on him. A kind of terror comes. There are too many people. How will he ever find friends, comrades, make a place for himself in the vast herd?

However, all boys do not leave their home towns. The boy whose father owns a grocery clerks in his father's store and later becomes a grocer. Or he goes away to college and comes back, sets up in his town as a doctor or lawyer. All his life he goes up and down along the same small town streets, past the same houses, meets the same men and women. The grown people he sees daily he knew when he wore his first pair of long pants, when he began going to the town school.

The town boy grows up, suddenly becomes a young man, begins going about with a small town girl, takes her to church and to dances and to the moving pictures. He takes her for a ride in the evening in his father's car and presently they are married. They have children. The small town man reads a city newspaper, listens to the radio. He is a Democrat or a Republican.

Friendships are formed. There are two men, who have known each other since boyhood, seen walking about together evening after evening. They talk. Of what can they be speaking? It may be that, after the beginning of such a friendship between two small town young men, one of them later goes away to some city, but he will never forget his small town friend. He will, all his life, remember vividly every house along the streets on which his father's house stood. It may be that, as a city man, he will never again form another friendship that will mean to him quite what his remembered small town friendship meant.

It was with that friend of his youth that he discussed all of his early problems and dreams. To him he confessed his first love, with him smoked his first cigarette, took his first drink of beer. How vividly he remembers the night when he and his friend went together to a nearby larger town. There was something they both wanted intensely or thought they wanted. They went together to a certain notorious house, stood trembling and ashamed before the house and then came away. They hadn't the courage to enter.

"Gee, Harry, I haven't got the nerve, have you?"

"No, Jim, I guess I've lost my nerve."

The doings of the big outside world are nowadays brought more and more to the small towners. The President speaks to them at the same moment he is speaking to the city man. There remains, both for the small towner and the city man, raised in an American small town, the memory of the sharing of the experiences, the dreams, the disappointments of youth. They both remember the time they went with the town ball team to play a team in a neighboring town. Together as boys they discussed the mysteries of life, of death, of love, of religion.

**Friendships are formed**

"Do you believe in God? What do you think, Harry?"

"Well, I don't know, Jim. When a fellow looks up at the sky at night—"

The city man remembers vividly his small town school teacher, the place where he with the other town boys built a dam in the creek to make a swimming hole. If he were from a Southern small town, he remembers a Negro boy with whom he went hunting coons or 'possum at night. The Northern boy remembers the hills on which he went bobsledding, the ponds on which he learned to skate. There was always another boy who could outskate him, who could cut figure eights and other fancy strokes. When he tried it, he kept falling.

Sometimes the city man, remembering an old hunger, returns to the town of his youth. He walks about the streets.

The town seems strangely changed to him. It is a constant shock to him that the people of his town have also grown older.

There is a gray-haired man he remembers as a slight youth who played shortstop on the baseball team. Perhaps the main street of his town has been paved since he was a boy. The whole town seems to have shrunk in size. He remembers the long journey when, as a child, he first set off to school. Now it seems but a step from the house where he spent his childhood to the school building.

The city man returning thus to his home town has always a feeling of sadness. He resents the changes in the town, the fact that people of the town have grown older as he has, that strangers have come in.

During all his life in the city, the small town of his boyhood has remained home to him. Every house in the town, the faces of people seen on the street in his boyhood, have all remained sharply in his mind. How clearly he remembers the hill above the water-works pond, where he, with a troupe of other boys, went along a path beside a wheat field to the town swimming hole. He remembers the way the wind played in the wheat. If he is a Southern boy he remembers the fall days when he gathered persimmons, the fires under the kettles where sorghum molasses was being made at night, Negro women skimming the yellow-green froth off the boiling juice.

Or the night when he with a boyhood friend walked home together from a dance or from a spelling bee at a country schoolhouse, the dusty dirt road along which they walked, the wind in the tall fall corn, the rustling sound when the wind played among the broad dry corn leaves, rubbing them together and making a sound like ghosts running whispering through the corn.

He remembers the town's haunted house, the night when he and several other town boys played "follow-your-leader" and a daring boy led them into the town graveyard.

How small and strange the town seems when he returns. He is shocked, half wishing he hadn't come. "It would have been better to let my dream, my memory, alone," he thinks.

But there is a realization in him also that the city in which he has been living for years is made up also of an infinite number of small towns.

There is something reached for, wanted also by the city man—to be known and recognized by the clerk in the neighboring drug store, the nearby A. & P., or the news dealer at the corner. He wants also to be known and recognized by the waiters in the city restaurant where he goes for his noonday lunch.

It is the old hunger for intimacy. As yet the great majority of American city men come from the small towns. They remember vividly the intimacy of life in the towns. Many of them remain, during all the years of their life as city men, at heart small-towners.

**All boys do not leave their home towns**

**Jeweller**, San Augustine, Texas

**Store Clerk,** San Augustine, Texas

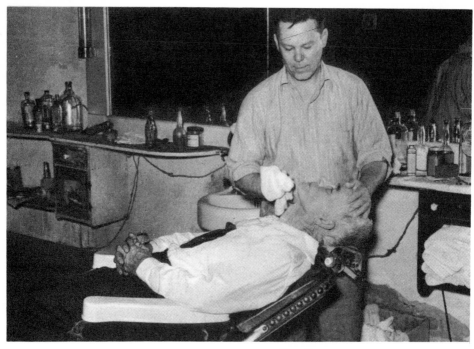

**Barber,** San Augustine, Texas

**County Clerk**, San Augustine, Texas

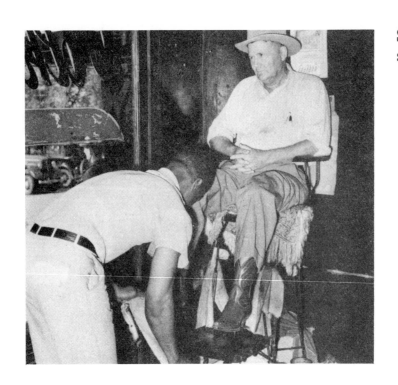

## Shoe Shine,
### San Augustine, Texas

## Shoe Repair, San Augustine, Texas

**Druggist,** San Augustine, Texas

**Constable,**
San Augustine, Texas

**Blacksmith,**
San Augustine,
Texas

**Teacher,**
San Augustine,
Texas

**General Store,** San Augustine, Texas

# IV

# SPRING HAS COME.

Spring is the time when the country comes most into the towns, is most felt in the towns. The winds bring the message from the fields into the towns.

Ed Prouse is now going up and down the main street with a paper for people to sign. Put your name down for a dollar if you are a prosperous man for two or three dollars. We want a baseball team this year. We've got to buy uniforms, bats and balls. If you are a merchant and pay for a uniform, a player will wear the name of your store printed in big letters on his uniform.

Plant hollyhocks along the alleyways. Trim the grapevines.

"Hell, my wife is cleaning house again. A man can't find a clean shirt, can't even find his razor."

"When the leaves on the maple trees are as big as squirrels' ears it is time to plant corn."

Windows of houses all over town thrown open now, bedding out on clotheslines, the new model cars coming in, mule markets in Kentucky, Tennessee, and Missouri.

"If I can raise the price I am going to trade in the old car this year."

A new aliveness in the main streets of the towns, more color in the windows of stores, spring term of court in county seat towns, a stir, an awakening, feel of earth invading the towns, smell of earth, new hope, warm spring rains, the vivid new green of grass on lawns before the houses, the children looking forward to the end of the school year, to swimming in the town's pond or in the creek, to barefoot days.

Spring is a never ceasing wonder in the towns, the drab days gone, a new beginning. Nowadays the almost universal owning of cars takes men more and more out of the towns into the country. Town kids can't wait

for the summer days to come. There are plenty of Tom Sawyers and Huckleberry Finns left in American towns. On the first sunny days there will be the daring ones who sneak off to the creek, pond or river, plunge in, come out shivering.

"Better get your hair dry before you go home. Ma will raise cain if she finds out you've been in."

Formerly, only twenty-five or thirty years ago, almost every American family had a hog pen in the back yard. In the spring the town man bought a young pig, the stench of the pens to poison the summer air, but that time has passed, although you will still see in the American town, up to five thousand people, cows being driven off to the field at the town's edge, mornings and evenings.

The great thing is the annual awakening, the apple, cherry, and peach trees coming into bloom. In the town men become for the time half farmer, earth men. There is fear of a late frost to nip the bloom, talk of that going on the streets, in the stores, when men gather in the town post offices for the morning mail. In the drug stores and the groceries the seed packages stand up in racks. They add a touch of color to the stores. The women gather about. They are planning their flower and vegetable gardens.

Hal Grimes, the house painter, is carrying on a little business on the side. In his back yard he has built row after row of boxes with glass covers, hot boxes for plants. He puts an ad in the town paper.

"Fine tomato and cabbage plants for sale."

Men and women are driving out to Hal's place in their cars. This is the busy time of the year for Hal, plenty of paper hanging and painting to do, but his wife is on the job. She has put on slacks and gloves to protect her hands. She is serving out the plants.

"They say Hal makes nearly two hundred dollars out of his plant business every spring."

Like all the other house painters and paper hangers, Hal has his hands full. The women nag at him.

"Hal's got a mighty fine wife. It's too bad he drinks."

In all the Northern towns the families that can go off South during the winter months, to live, during the winter months, in trailer or tourist camps in Florida or California, are coming home now. You see the great drift of cars, like swallows flying north in the spring.

Tall tales being told.

"How much did it cost you to live down there?"

"I wish I could get out of here in the winter. I can't. I've got my store, I've got my law practice. I can't take my kids out of school."

Life in the towns spreading out in a new way, the old tight close life broken up by the coming of the new big paved highways, the streams of cars always flowing through the towns, endless rivers of cars, American restlessness.

Now the young blades of the town are all wanting new spring suits, the girls new spring dresses. There is a restlessness that gets into the blood. Now you see young couples on spring evenings walking slowly along streets with hands clasped together. June will be a great time for marriages.

"I want we should live together, have a house of our own, like a man and woman should."

The young ones drive about in the family cars, sit together beside the country road, on quiet streets under the trees on moonlit spring nights, the young corn just thrusting through the earth in nearby fields, in the South in nearby fields the young cotton, problems of the young, in the towns as in the cities, how to get started, get going, set up new families, keep the old town life going.

"Sometimes I think I'll have to join the army, get out of here."

"Gee, I'd hate that, Jim, I'd miss you so much."

In every town there is the slipshod lazy man who won't clean up his place in the spring. He is slovenly and has a slovenly wife. His back yard is full of old broken boxes and tin cans. He won't clean it up. He is an individualist.

"Hell, I've got the spring fever. Whether I clean up my yard or not is my own business."

It is the time of new hope in the towns, the ever recurring miracle, changing the face of the towns. East, West, North, and South, the song of new life up out of the soil, in the towns men coming out of their walled-in winter life, strolling in the town streets, neighbor calling to neighbor.

"Spring is here."

New gladness in the voices of young and old.

Another spring.

"Spring is here."

V

HOT SUMMER DAYS HAVE COME, with summer rains in the far South, along the Gulf Coast and in the Ohio and Missouri river valleys. The hot days and the warm sticky nights come now to towns in the river valleys. In little Louisiana river towns and in towns along the Gulf Coast there is the loud sustained song of insect life. A man is lying asleep in his house in a Louisiana town. Frogs croak loudly in the nearby bayous. He gets out of bed, takes the sheets off his bed, soaks them in the bathtub or under the water tap in the kitchen and puts them back on the bed. He hopes to get to sleep while the water is evaporating, cooling the air in the room.

In the cotton country, young Negro men and women are now out in the streets at night. In the Negro section of Southern towns you hear the soft voices and the laughter of Negroes. Old Negro men and women sit on the porches of the little unpainted houses in the long afternoons and in the summer nights. At night Negro children play under the corner street lights.

In the Southern cotton mill towns men and women are going in and out of the mill gate and along the hot streets of the nearby company-owned mill town. Although it may be on level ground the mill village is always spoken of as "The Hill."

Our country is a land of violent changes in climate. Hot winds come up from the Southwest to blow over Iowa, Nebraska, and Kansas. The hot winds cross the great river into the states of the Middlewest. In the fields near the towns there is a curious rustling of the long blades of the growing corn.

Now you will hear corn talk in all the corn shipping towns of the Middlewest. The hot winds do not hurt the corn. Men call to each other on the streets of the towns.

"This is corn growing weather all right."

It is time now for the small town people to be out of doors. In most of the countries of an old European world the summer life of the people in the towns is led in gardens back of the houses but here, in North America, we live during the hot months at the front of the house. We live on the front porch.

We live on the front porch

The people of the towns sit in groups on their front porches. In the warm darkness, on summer evenings, there is a movement from house to house, visits made back and forth, low-voiced talk going on. But a few years ago the stores on Main Street were open until ten or eleven at night but nowadays, with the exception of the drug store and the town restaurants, the stores are closed at six. Main Street becomes a place of strollers, of sitters in parked cars, of groups gathered for talk.

In the street older men stand about or sit on store window ledges. Story telling and political discussions go on. Occasionally an argument develops and a fight starts. The married man of the small town is seldom at home on summer evenings. When he doesn't take the family to the movies, he gets up from the evening meal and reaches for his hat.

"I guess I'll step down town for awhile."

Or the mother of a family, when her children do not demand it, is out in the family car. She picks up a woman friend. They park the car on Main Street and sit and watch the life of the street. The youngsters who are not now sitting on darkened porches, hand holding, doing their courting, drift up and down the main street into the drug store and the town movie house.

In the breakup that came to America in '29 many well-to-do men in American towns got caught. Like the city men they had gone stock-market wild. In towns all over America there were merchants, professional men, bankers, many of whom had saved carefully for years, who went into the market. They suddenly became dreamers, dreaming of getting suddenly, miraculously rich. They went down in the crash and the sons and daughters they had planned to send to college were out looking for jobs. They helped to swell the army of the jobless.

After the big break in '29 when the C. C. C. camps began to be scattered over the country, absorbing some of the young men out of work, there were many state parks built over the country. Nowadays, when almost every American family has managed to hang on to some kind of a car, what is a matter of fifty, sixty, or even a hundred miles if you can raise the price of the gas? The car is the last thing the American family, gone broke, will part with. Some of them will sell their beds first and sleep on the floor. Car ownership means freedom to move about, it means standing in the town life. To the young men of the towns it means you get a girl to go out with you or you don't.

Always now, through the long summer days and through summer evenings, the rivers of cars flow through the towns. At night the headlights of the cars make a moving stream of light. If there is a big highway passing through the town, the streets are lined with tourist houses and tourist camps have been built at the town's edge. On summer nights as you lie on your bed in your house in the American town, you hear the heavy rumble of goods trucks. If there is a steep grade through your town the heavily loaded trucks, in low gear, shake the walls of your house. The man who once owned the town hardware store or who is a cashier in the town bank and went broke in '29, still owns a big brick house. There is a sign in the street before his house. "Tourist Home" the sign says.

The girls who work in cotton mills and live in cotton mill towns and can't afford to own cars, hire a truck, crowd into it and go off picnicking to the woods or swimming in some lake on Saturday afternoons. Summer is the time for the circus to come to town. Even American towns of less than five thousand have golf courses and tennis courts. There is a growing passion for flower gardens. On Sunday afternoon the small town man gets his car out. His wife and children pile in and they join the great parade—America on the move. The summer days won't last too long.

It is the time of mosquitoes, of summer rains, of hot still week-days on Main Street, no coal bills, greens from the garden, roasting ear time. Who has the first sweet corn, whose tomatoes ripen first, what girls will get married this summer? Life in the town during the long summer days and weeks relaxes. In the Dakotas and down through Kansas, Nebraska, northern Texas, and in the far West it is wheat harvesting time. It is hay cutting, wheat harvesting time in the small farms about New England and Middlewestern towns.

Hot dusty days, long days, summer rains—the summer days are the best of all the year's days for the American small towner.

Main Street becomes
a place of strollers...

...of groups gathered for talk

Hot dusty days

**Long days**

**Still week days...**

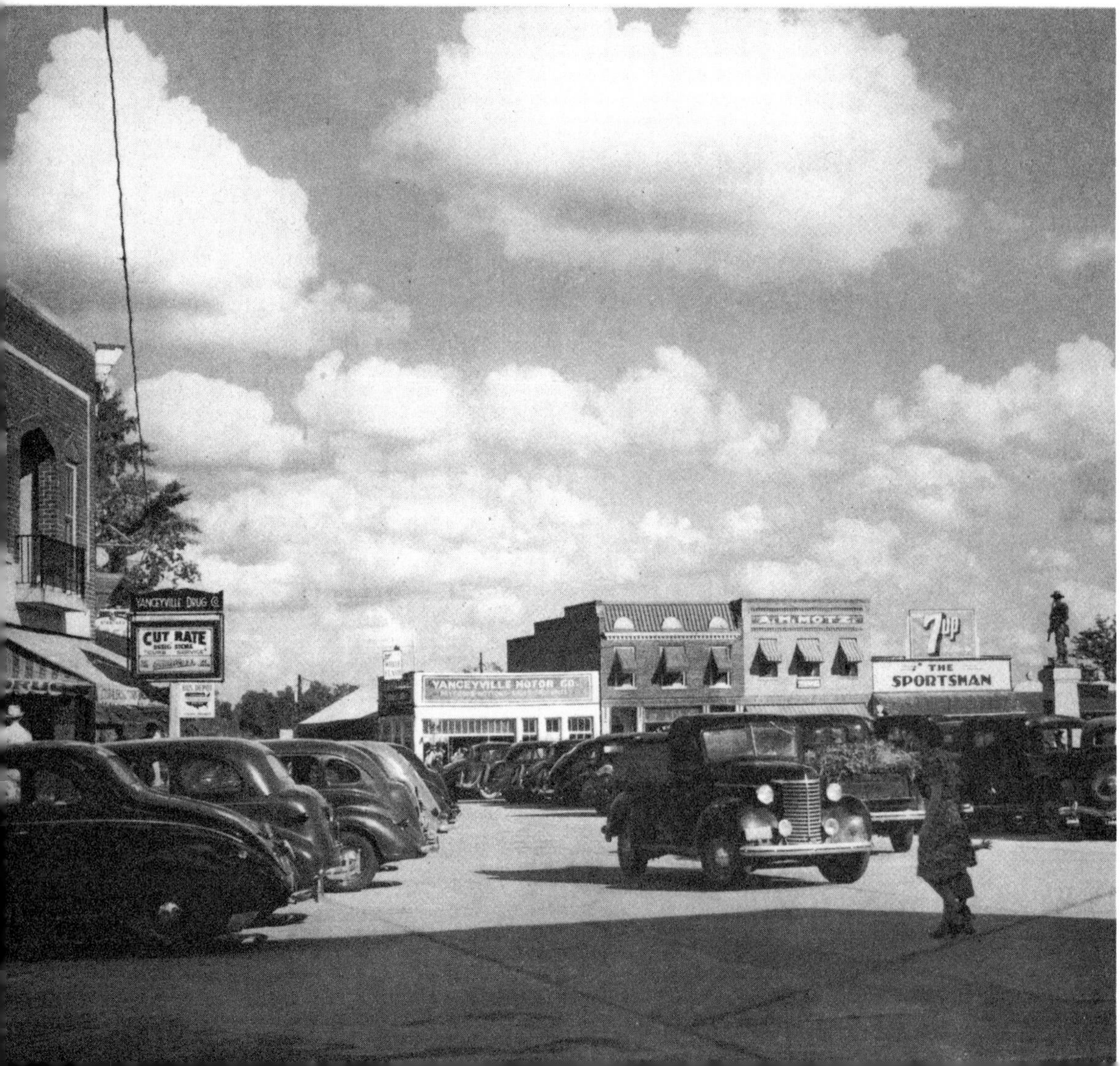

## ...On Main Street

## VI

IN THE TOWNS THE FALL IS the checking up time, the harvesting of the year's efforts of the American man to survive, getting a little forward in life. To the poor it brings dread of the long cold days of the North, the rain and mud of the South. Now in the gardens back of the houses in the towns the potato and tomato vines are withered and blackened. Men and women walk with a new soberness along the streets. In many hearts there is a creeping fear.

"How are we ever going to get through the winter, keep warm, feed and clothe the children?" a small town wife says to her husband.

In Southern towns now the trucks and wagons piled high with the newly-picked cotton stand waiting their turn at the small town cotton gins. Along the roads leading into town, weeds, bushes, and trees are decorated with clinging bunches of cotton. Soon the rows of baled cotton will be standing in the vacant lot about the gin or on the freight station platform. They will go off to the Southern mill towns or to the compresses in nearby cities to be squeezed small for shipment abroad. Great trucks, piled high with bales, are running along Southern highways and through Southern towns. Formerly the cotton went by wagon to the nearest river steamboat landing, river towns having a boom time, songs of the Negro stevedores floating up from river boats.

It is settlement time in the Southern towns, the tenant farmers of the South, white, black and brown, come in to check up on the year's work. There is the eternal hope of a little money coming in. The land owners have stood good for the tenants at the town stores, fertilizer bought in the spring, a tenant farmer allowed a little credit for fat-back and meal during the year. It is Tobacco Road come to town.

Men, women and children of the Southern towns, white and black, go out into the fields for the fall cotton picking, children wanting shoes, the men new overalls, the women new dresses. The cotton crop and the price it brings is a vital story to them.

The coming South of the cotton mills brought hordes of the poor tenant farmers into the towns. Often the mill seems the town's one hope. Stock in some of the mills was sold by the preachers in the churches. It was done with prayer in which the whole town joined, hoped-for employment, a little actual money coming in, often a chance for some sort of education for the children in the mill town schools.

In the upper South in the fall the tobacco markets are opened in the towns, in the Sugar Belts down Louisiana way, it is the time of cane cutting. The big cane mills are pressing out the juice from the cane. You see the children of the towns, white and black, each sucking away at a joint of cane.

The tobacco markets enliven the streets of the town in the tobacco country, in Virginia, North Carolina, Kentucky, and Tennessee. The tobacco buyers, shrewd fast-working men, have come to town. They are living in the town hotel. They seem like supermen to the tobacco growers. They are to make the price for the year's tobacco crop. In the evening they go together to the movies or sit together in a hotel room playing cards. It is hard to convince the tobacco growers and town people that they do not get together on prices. When prices are down you hear people along the street growling at them as they go back and forth to the big warehouses.

"Hey you, how much tobacco you going to steal today?"

There are huge trucks loaded with the tobacco in "hands" coming into town. Little broken down trucks climb painfully the steep grade into town in the hill country. Automobiles have tobacco piled high in the back seat.

It is a nervous waiting time. Here again, when the towns of the upper South have not become factory towns, the whole year's chances for prosperity hang on the price the crop brings, on the condition of the crop. Everything counts in making the price—the color, the texture of the leaf. In the light-yellow tobacco country of North Carolina and in

52

Tidewater, Virginia, the tobacco is kiln dried but in the burley country of southwest Virginia, Kentucky, and Tennessee it is cured in big tobacco barns or sun cured on poles in the field.

A hail storm on the growing tobacco can ruin it. Not too many growers know the secret of grading. They mix the bad with the good, the rain-splashed leaves at the base of the plant, called "ground lugs," with the broad clean leaves out of the center of the plant's middle and the whole crop goes off at a low price. In the big tobacco warehouses of the towns there is the sustained, queerly Oriental chant of the auctioneers. Farmers wait about for their turn to get their tobacco on the sales floor. They stand by the loaded trucks, lined up in the town streets. They wait on the warehouse floor anxiously watching as the prices go up and down. Where there is a big market, farmers sleep on their loads in the town streets.

The growers stand about in the streets of the town. Wives and children stand waiting. There is a curious intensity in faces. Merchants of the town also wait anxiously. Will it be a good or a bad year?

The buyers for the big tobacco and cigarette companies are going up and down pulling hands out of the great baskets, making their bids. They become temporarily half gods, deciding the fate of growers and town men alike.

54

**Huge trucks,
little trucks,
automobiles—
piled high with tobacco**

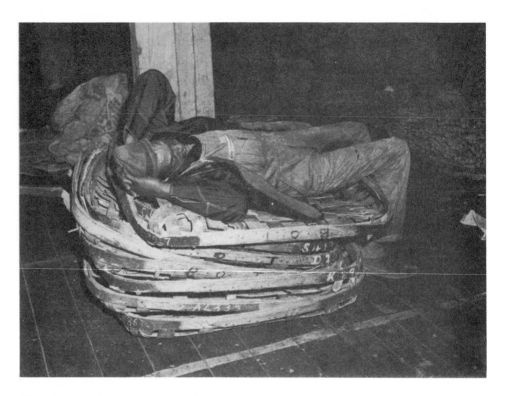

**Farmers sleep on their loads...**

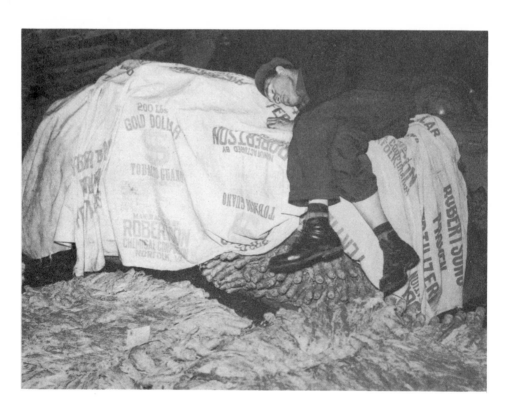

The price for the year's crop

What the cotton crop means to the towns of the lower South and tobacco to the upper South the potato crop means to the communities in the northern New England states, to Colorado and Idaho, the apple crop to north Pacific Coast towns and to the valleys of Virginia.

In the Middlewest it is corn cutting time and at the edge of some of the towns, corn husking contests are held. Champion corn huskers come to town to win prizes. Trucks loaded with yellow corn run swiftly through the streets of Middlewestern towns, some of the yellow ears falling in the streets. There are yellow ears, fallen from trucks, along the sides of roads leading into town. In some of the states the corn shocks stand like armies on parade. In other states they break the ears out of the stalks and turn the cattle into the fields. On still nights in little towns you hear the crash of cattle among the dry standing corn in nearby fields. When the corn is shocked you see the piles of gold against the brown earth.

Although the coming of the factories has changed life tremendously in many small American towns the greater number of them are still tied to the soil, hay prices, cattle prices, cabbage, wheat, corn, oats, potato prices, abundance or failure of crop, prices the crops bring, tell the story of hard or good times in the towns.

The fall is the time for the town boys to go nut gathering in the woods, the hunters to clean their guns and go into the fields with their bird and rabbit dogs.

Apples to be picked and cider made, the women of the little frame houses of the towns doing their fall canning.

Only a generation or two ago in all the smaller American towns a hog was kept in a pen in the back yard but now the town man, instead of killing his own hog, goes out into the country and buys a pole hog. There is lard and sausage making, hams and slabs of bacon are hung up to be cured. For the most part the old fashioned family cellar with its bins of apples and potatoes, its long rows of fruits in glass jars on shelves is disappearing. There is more dependence on the canned goods bought in stores, put up by the big canneries. The town man is a little less close to the life of the farms but with the coming of tight times there is, in many small towns, a going back to old ways.

In the houses of the town when fall comes the radios bring the result of the baseball world series and the big football games. High school boys are being put through football practice on the playground back of the town high school building. Where is your American small town, in the coal mining country, in the North, South, East, or West without its high school football team? If a town boy shows up well, has speed and power, he may be able to make football carry him through some big state college or university. It happens.

In the coal mining towns the mines have speeded up production. In the late summer and fall the roar of coal down the tipple goes on all day long, a black dust settling over the towns, winds carrying it over nearby fields, dimming the fall colors in trees. It is in your hair, your nose, your eyes, your clothes. An increasingly big amount of coal is carried away from the mine towns in trucks, over hundreds of miles of paved highways, to towns outside the mining section. The fall is the time for strikes, for a tightening up of the labor front. As in the Southern cotton mill towns, the houses in which the miners live are owned by the companies that operate the mines.

The fall is election time in the towns. The politicians are about, often going from house to house, shaking hands with the men, caressing babies, making promises.

Can a man make the old overcoat last through another year, can he get new shoes for the kids, will the town factory run full-handed this year, what about the price of coal, can the wife make the old cookstove stand up through another winter?

"I tell you what, Jake, I wish I was one of the lucky ones. I wish I could put the family in the old car, go off south to Florida or west to California. I wonder if we will ever have real prosperity back again, plenty of jobs, plenty of work for a man to do?"

"Say, have you put anti-freeze in your car yet?"

"Gee, but the summer seemed short. Seems like a wind just blew it away."

Fall: West Virginia

## Fall: Mississippi

**Fall: Iowa**

all: Vermont

## VII

IN THE TOWNS, WINTER, FOR ALL the radios and the movies, is the waiting time. It is the time between for the American small towner. In spite of the spread of factories to the towns, North and South, the American small town remains close to the life of the land. The land sleeps and waits and the towns wait.

In the far Northern states of New England and up through the Northwest the bitter cold days come early, the spring with its new beginning is far away. Weatherwise old men have been up and down the Main Streets making predictions. They say that all of the animals have put on a thick coat of fur. It will be a long hard winter. In Southern towns, on Saturday afternoons, country men, Negroes and whites, come into the towns bringing loads of firewood. They come in one-mule wagons or in worn-out trucks, to stand about the town square, patiently waiting for buyers. In some of the towns public markets have been built. The country women bring in their canned goods, potatoes and cabbage. They sit in their little booths wrapped in heavy overcoats. Now the road men of the North get out the snow moving machinery. The big highways that run through the towns must be kept clear. The cars must move. America must keep rolling.

In the early winter in the towns, all over America, Christmas decorations go up along Main Street, the store windows take on a new gaiety, wreaths of evergreen are hung on the doorknobs of houses, the local weekly is full of Christmas advertisements. You go up to the high school to watch the high school football team in a game with the boys of some nearby town, stand about shivering, only, alas, too often, to see your home town boys get a licking. You get the flu. You get through Thanksgiving, eat your share of turkey, if you can afford one.

You get all of your relatives in, have a big feast, get into an argument with your brother-in-law. He is a Republican and you are a Democrat.

The argument gets hot, becomes a quarrel, and your wife tries to patch it up, to make peace. Very likely when your brother-in-law has gone angrily away, you get down-the-river from your wife.

It is small town life. You have to go on living with people day after day, week after week. You can't just ignore your brother-in-law, forget him as you might in a city. Tomorrow you will meet him on the street. You will be meeting him in the stores and in the post office. Better make it up, start over again.

It is the old problem of living with men, finding a common ground on which you can stand with your fellows, this intensified in the towns.

Now is the time to go skating. The boys have taken up the new sport of skiing. If there is a hill near town it is time to get out the bob-sleds.

"Jake, do you remember the old days when Al Wright kept the livery stable? Do you remember how he used to keep a couple of pretty good trotters? He got them out when the sleighing was good. He and Doc Payne, who owned that big blind pacer, and Judge Crawford with his little sorrel, would be having it lickety-split up and down Main Street."

"Yes, and the farmers with their bob-sleds coming into town, the boys flipping on, stealing a ride, parties we used to go on out to some farmer's house or to a barn dance."

"I'll tell you what, Ike, I don't know sometimes whether all these modern inventions we've got are a good thing or not."

There used to be show troupes come into the towns in the winters, the actors walking on the streets in the afternoons. The movies killed them off. Every winter a burlesque show came. Only the men went to that. It was called a "leg show." Going was a nice wicked thing to do.

America must keep rolling

66

# A hill near town

The towns wait

the towns sleep

The Christmas tree has been brought in from the woods and set up in the parlor. Some of the more well-to-do have set up trees in the front yards. They are covered with small many-colored electric lights. In Southern towns they shoot off firecrackers. Tourists come back to the Northern towns in the spring and tell about it. "They make a Fourth of July out of Christmas down there," they say. The Five and Tens have done a booming business. The churches hold special Christmas services. Some of them have Christmas trees and kids who have been regular attendants at Sunday School through the year get their reward.

Over most of America the real winter comes after Christmas. It may be that the town's women's club gets up a lecture course. They canvass the town selling tickets. This is where we get our culture. You've got to buy a season ticket and go to show you're cultured. It is the women who keep up the cultural tone for us. College boys come with their glee clubs and sing in the town hall, the court house or in one of the churches. Miss Grayson, who is unmarried but wrote a book on how to live a happy married life, comes and lectures to us, a magician comes and does his tricks.

Some of our more cultured women, our local literati, have formed a book club. The druggist's wife who went to Smith College reviews the latest best seller. The high school boys have a basket-ball team, there is always the radio and the movies and in the back of Cal Hurd's shoe repair shop there is a checker game going on.

Upstairs over the bank in Fred Travey's law office on dismal winter afternoons you can get into a poker game if you are looking for sport. Better look out. Fred and Theodore Shovely, the coal and lumber dealer, will clean you out.

In every American town, as in our cities, there is a section beyond the railroad tracks where the poor live. We in the towns also have our slums. In the summer and fall the men who live down there manage to pick up a day's work now and then but in the winter there is nothing doing. There are a half dozen children in the family and the mother tries to keep things going by doing the washing for our well-to-do families. You will see her on bitter cold days hanging out a wash. Her hands are blue with cold. In the houses the children huddle about the one stove in the kitchen, wood and coal to be bought, shoes for the children. It is a long winter for that family. The woman who is hanging out the washed clothes is a proud one. She'll work her arms off, she says, rather than go on relief. The long depression, unemployment, has killed the spirit of more than one such woman. They have had to throw in the sponge, give it up. They couldn't make it.

In the winter the small town doctors, East and West, North and South, are up and out day and night, through mud and snow. There are babies to be delivered, people down with the flu. Since the depression and the end of prohibition the small town lawyer finds the pickings thinner. There are too many people hard up. They can't afford to take their quarrels into court. The small town doctors have a hard time collecting their bills.

There is the weekly meeting of the Kiwanis and the Rotary Clubs. Some of the so-called "service clubs" meet for dinner in the evening at the town hotel. It gives the men a chance to make speeches, tell the others what is the matter with the town.

"We ought to get more factories," the speakers keep saying.

On lodge nights the women pick up a "snack" and go off to the movies. In many towns, no matter how small, there is a women's card club. Only the more well-to-do are invited into that.

There is a dance on Saturday night, country girls coming into town with their beaus. If there is a factory in the town the factory hands go. There are revivals being held in the churches. In the very small town the church becomes the center of social life. The church women will be giving suppers to raise money to help pay the preacher. In the South a little unpainted wooden Negro church fills the winter lives of the town Negroes. There are cries and shouts, a swaying of brown bodies, a rhythmic beating of feet on cold wooden floors, something released, the pent up emotions of a race.

Winter is, in a curious way, the test time for the people of the towns, the test of men's and women's ability to live together. There is that brother-in-law with whom you had a quarrel. You and he made it up. You have quarrels with other men, even sometimes with the wife. You have to forget it, start over again. It is the only way you can make life livable when you must go on with the same people day after day, during the long winter months.

The women who keep up...

...our cultural tone

You've got to buy
a season ticket...

...to show
you're cultured

The weekly meeting of
the "Service Clubs"

## VIII

THE WELL-KNOWN SMALL TOWN individualist is an established figure in American life. He is in the cities as in the small town but in the small town you know him. Curious enough characters out of life no doubt pass you by the thousands in the city streets but they come and go swiftly. You do not meet them day after day in the same streets, the same stores. You do not talk with them, know intimately their idiosyncrasies.

In every American small town there is the lonely man who seldom leaves his own house. Usually he is a bachelor. He has let a high hedge grow about the yard almost hiding his house from the street. There are always whispered stories floating about the town concerning his life in the house. It is said that as a young man he was rejected by a beautiful woman. We Americans are born romanticists. Often there are more dark menacing tales. In his youth it is said that he committed some mysterious crime. It may be that he came suddenly into town from another place. Year after year his house remains unpainted. The yard before the house is overgrown with weeds. The front porch is rotting away. Occasionally he is seen emerging from his house at night. He hurries furtively along streets. He continually talks to himself.

Sid Smith is the practical joker of the town. He loves to send the town's half-wit on fool errands. He sends him to the hardware store for a left-handed monkey-wrench, to the print shop to see the type lice. He is the fellow who hands out loaded cigars that blow up in your face. When he has been successful with one of his victims he runs up and down Main Street telling the story, boasting of his cleverness.

The man who loves an argument is down town on Main Street every afternoon and evening. When he sees a group of men talking together, he joins them. He goes from group to group listening to talk and when a statement is made he immediately challenges it.

He grows angry, he shouts. His wife is always scolding him.

"Why are you always making enemies? Why do you do it?"

He doesn't know why. He keeps making up his mind that he will be calm and quiet, talk quietly to others. He can't do it. On the next day he is at it again. He would really like to be a quiet sensible fellow, leading a quiet sensible life.

In every town there is the woman who is always having operations. She goes from one doctor to another. Almost everything has been cut out of her. She has grown pale and walks with difficulty, but she is a proud woman. She thinks of herself as a figure in the community. There isn't another woman in town who has been through what she has, she keeps declaring. She is one who enjoys her own suffering.

And there is always that other woman, a born nurse. She is a fat jolly soul. When someone is sick she comes to help. She is always Aunt Molly, or Kate, or Sarah, is everyone's aunt. She spreads cheer, has the touch.

And the school teacher who never marries although she was such a fine looking younger woman. She goes on, year after year, teaching new crops of children. She has won the respect of the town but remains, all her life, an oddly lonely-seeming figure.

Henry Horner is the town butt. He is a man of forty-five and his wife is dead. He lives with his wife's sister in a house out at the edge of town.

Henry once had a little money and went into business. He became a chicken fancier and concocted a chick food to put on the market. He went from town to town trying to sell it but did not succeed. He spent all his money in the venture.

Now Henry dresses shabbily and has let his hair grow long. He carries a heavy cane and as he goes through the streets of the town boys crow at him. They imitate the cackle of hens that have been at the business of laying eggs and the clarion cry of the rooster. Henry grows violently angry. He waves his cane about, he swears, he pursues the boys furiously but never catches them. As he passes through Main Street some man, standing in a group of men by the post office, also crows. Henry approaches the group. His hands are trembling. He stands before them demanding justice.

"What man of you did that?"

All the men of the group shake their heads. They look at Henry with blank faces. The town has discovered his weakness. There is a cruel streak in men. They cannot let poor Henry live his life in peace.

A young girl of the town has gone wrong early in life. Some man or boy has got her and has gone about telling the story. Other men and boys begin the pursuit. She is always lying about with men and boys, in fields near the town or in the town graveyard. Hers is a story as old as the Bible. In the town graveyard there is a crude and brutal expression of the meeting of life and death.

Thaddeus is the town's philosopher. He is respected by all the town. The word is out that he is well-read. It is even said that he knows Latin and Greek. Every evening he sits at home reading a book. His wife is a scold but he pays no attention to her. The men of the town speak of him with admiration and envy.

"Gee, I wish I had his education."

Thaddeus is a quiet serene man who is deeply religious, although he never goes to church. He has worked out his own notion of God. He is a merchant who also owns a farm near town and is fond of young boys. He is very gentle with them. He has no children of his own but, on summer afternoons, he is always taking some boy with him to his farm. Once he caught a clerk stealing money in his store. He did not discharge the clerk.

He is a mystic. "God," he says to the boy who has ridden with him to the farm, "is in the growing corn. He is in the trees over there in that wood, in the grass in that meadow, in the flowering weeds along the road." The boy does not understand but feels happy in the presence of the quiet smiling man.

There is the town bully. He is forever boasting of fights he has won. He goes swaggering about with a half-burned cigar in the corner of his mouth. He declares he has never lost a fight.

"I'll knock your block off. I'll bust your jaw," he is always shouting to some one. It is the tradition of the towns that he always in the end meets his match. Some smaller man, infuriated by his insults, lights into him and beats him up. It always happens and when it does it fills the town with joy.

A mysterious woman comes to town. She appears suddenly and rents a house in a quiet residence street. She is one who keeps to herself, makes no acquaintances. When she appears in the street, she is always well-dressed. All sorts of whispered stories about her run through the town. Young boys hear the stories and walk far out of their way going to and from school to pass her house.

The shades are always drawn and the town is convinced that she is a wicked sinful woman. There is a story that she has some connection with a mysterious band of robbers.

Or it is said that she is a kept woman, that she is being kept by a rich man of some distant city. A man of the town who lives on her street declares that often, after midnight, a big expensive-looking car parks before her house and a man enters. To the young boys of the town she becomes a symbol of something strange and enticing, out of some mysterious world of sin. It is said that in her house there are luxurious carpets and expensive furniture, that she wears jewels that have cost thousands of dollars. The woman stays for a time in the house and then disappears as mysteriously as she came. She also remains in the town's imagination a figure of romance.

Arthur is a thin wiry little man who is always gay. No matter how gloomy the day he is full of good cheer. He knows everyone, cries gaily to others as he hurries through the streets. He goes with a half dancing step.

"Hello! Hello!"

"How are you feeling, Art?"

"Fine! Fine!"

Arthur is as full of life as a squirrel. He hops and dances. Something inside him is always singing and dancing. He is gay, alive, small, an always cheerful streak of sunlight on the town's streets.

There is the man who goes with the same woman year after year. He goes to see her every Sunday evening, takes her to church, drives about with her on week-day evenings in his car. He is always at her house on one or two evenings during the week, sits with her on the porch of her house. He began going with her when he and she were both in high school. That was nineteen or twenty years ago. He has never paid any attention to any other woman nor has she ever been with any other man. When she began going with him she was quite pretty but now she begins to look a little worn. Her mother has died and she is keeping house for her father. The people of the town see the couple going about together year after year. They are a little amused. The word is out that they are engaged. Nothing happens. He just continues to go with her year after year.

There is always the town's stingy man. People say that he gives Abraham Lincoln a headache the way he squeezes a penny. All American towns have a flare for nicknames. He is called Penny Smith, or Penny Jones.

He has a little store at the end of Main Street where he sells nick-nacks. It is called a Variety Store.

"Do you know what — I was in Penny Smith's store. He had dropped a penny on the floor. Several customers came in but he paid no attention to them. They grew tired of waiting and went out. He was down on his knees behind the counter looking for the penny he had dropped. I could have walked off with everything in the store and he wouldn't have known it. He was too absorbed in finding that penny."

There is a young man who was once called the bright boy of the town. In school he took all of the prizes. His father sent him to college. He was the top man in his classes.

He came home and set up as a lawyer or doctor in the town and presently married. He married a daughter of one of the more well-to-do men of the town. He went along, a steady successful quiet man until he was forty.

And then suddenly he went to pieces. Until he was forty he had never been known to take a drink.

Then he began. He took bottles of whisky up into his office, was seen on many afternoons reeling through the streets. No one knows what happened to him. He was one kind of man one day and almost on the next day he became something else.

Now he is the town drunkard and his wife has a frightened look on her face. No one knows what made him do it. It is not explainable, something that fills the town with awe.

Carl is the small town man who has the gift. He may have been the son of one of the more well-to-do citizens of the town or he may have been a poor man's son. It doesn't matter. Carl was one, destined from birth, to get on in the world. If he had been a big city man or had lived in one of the industrial cities he might have become a captain of industry, a millionaire. In his own town he does well enough.

Often he has no particular business, goes to no office. He walks about, making trades, he lends money, trades in real estate. Dollars stick to his fingers. Every year, in hard times and good times, he keeps getting ahead. He is one who has the gift, who never overlooks a chance. To the people of the town, he seems a good-natured quiet fellow but he is not very inclined to make friends. The town secretly admires him.

And then there is the man who throws it away. He keeps inheriting money from dying relatives but he cannot keep it. He had ten thousand dollars from an aunt who died in Kansas. Every time he makes an investment something goes wrong with it. He buys a house and forgets to take out insurance and on the next day it burns. He has several well-to-do relatives and keeps inheriting money but always it slips away from him.

There is a Carrie Nation in almost every American town. She takes it upon her shoulders to look after the town morals. She is always accusing others of some mysterious sin. During the time of prohibition she became a powerful figure. She was always telephoning to the sheriff, accusing some man of making or selling liquor. A young man is walking along the street smoking a cigarette and she stops before him. She stamps her foot, scolds at him.

"Take that cigarette out of your mouth, you filthy thing," she cries.

She is against the use of tobacco in all forms, against the drinking of any kind of intoxicants, against boys playing baseball or swimming on Sunday, against card playing. She hates all kinds of expressions of gaiety or joy, is down on dancing. She declares dancing leads young girls straight to ruin. She goes to see the girls' mothers, haunts the town editor. The whole weight of the town's moral life is on her shoulders.

The characters of the towns give the towns their color. In the small towns you know every man's idiosyncrasies. They cannot escape you. Life in the towns can be at times terrible or it can be infinitely amusing and absorbing.

The life in the town is a test of man's ability to adjust himself. It tells the story of his skill in living with others, his ability to go out to others and to let others be a part of his own life. You have to go on living with your neighbors. If they are sometimes queer it may be that they also think of you as queer. Without quite knowing it, you may yourself be one of the "characters of your town."

## IX

JOHN McNUTT HAS BEEN caught stealing chickens. He is an old offender. John lives out at the edge of town in the little shack down behind the gully that is the town dump. He owns an old half-ton truck and has several kids. He has been in jail many times and this time has been caught red-handed. Three of his kids, half-wild little creatures, were with him when they raked him in.

This worries John. He is afraid the little boys will also be put in jail or sent to a reform school. He pleads with the trial judge.

"Sure I'm guilty but my boys aren't." He declares that the boys did not know what he was up to and they are let off. John is sentenced to three months' work on the roads and the crowd of small towners gathered to hear the trial move out of the little courtroom.

The sheriff, two deputies, the trial judge, and the town editor remain.

They have a talk with John and he tells them how he worked.

"I send the kids out," he explains. "I have them carry fish poles on their shoulders or, in the fall, bags for gathering nuts and in the winter a pair of skates. I have spotted some farmer who has a lot of chickens I can get at. I send the kids to hang about his place. If he has a dog they try to coax him to follow. They throw him bones and pieces of meat. Then when we go back there at night maybe they can keep the dog quiet.

"I station the kids at night where they can watch and give the alarm. I'm an expert at this business, a good workman. I can lift a hen off the roost without her making a sound. The kids and I carry them away to where we have the truck hidden in a nearby woods. By the next morning I have the chickens sold in some town a hundred miles away."

John is pleased with himself. He grins at his listeners.

"Well, you caught me this time all right. One of my kids, I had hid along that road when you came up on me, went to sleep. You fellows have to admit that I have been a good workman on my job all right."

The trial judge, the deputies, and the newspaper man are grinning at John.

"Well, I guess I'll get plenty of exercise breaking them stones on the road," he says as they lead him away.

Since the players rarely come now to the small towns the court becomes the theater of the towns. What amusing, often tragic stories, come out into the light. In many of our states there are elected justices of the peace who try all the minor cases. The justice may be a farmer or any ordinary citizen of the town. He is a man who buys and sells cattle and hogs, or a small town real estate dealer. The petty thieves are brought before him. Sometimes two or three justices sit in on a case.

In a good many states our justices work on the fee system. If the man brought into court is cleared they get no fee and it is pretty hard to escape a fine, with "costs" in such a court.

The cow of a well-to-do farmer has got over into Ed Wyatt's cornfield and he hauls the farmer into court. Ed is a renter. You can't get a cent out of him but he is always lawing someone. The farmer offered Ed five dollars for the damage done to his little corn patch but Ed wouldn't take it. He wanted twenty-five, wanted to gouge the man. His claim is absurd but Ed is a notorious trouble maker. There are two justices sitting on the case. They decide to send two or three citizens out to look at Ed's corn patch and estimate the damage. Presently they return.

"Three dollars would be a generous settlement," they say.

The justices put the cost of the trial on the farmer and he protests.

"But I offered him five dollars. He brought this case into court, I didn't. I'll gladly pay the three dollars damages but I don't see why I should be stuck for the costs."

The two justices take the farmer aside.

"The trouble is that we can't get a cent out of Ed," they explain. "We've got to have three dollars apiece for our fee."

One of the justices gets an idea.

"I'll tell you what we'll do," he says. "We'll award Ed three dollars damages and one of us will keep that. Then we'll divide the cost, sticking you and Ed three dollars apiece. You pay another three dollars and that will make up the six dollars. You've already offered Ed five. This way you pay one dollar more and Ed doesn't get a cent."

The farmer is a little puzzled. He scratches his head. Then he gets the idea and grins.

"O. K.," he says, "Anyway it's a chance to put one over on Ed."

There is a crowd of country people gathered about the courthouse and loafing on the courthouse lawn. It is a county seat town and the circuit court is in session. For several days the court has been busy with so-called "civil cases," cases concerned with suits for damages, the location of the line between two farms, the responsibility for an automobile accident. A team of mules, loose in the road, have wandered into a railroad right-of-way and have been killed and the owner had sued the railroad. But now it is time for the criminal court cases to come up. Many witnesses have been summoned. They are town people and country people gathered in, often a little frightened and nervous. It may be that there is even a murder case to be tried and there is a waiting tenseness in the people.

The sheriff appears and stands at the top of the courthouse steps.

"Hear yees! Hear yees!" he calls. His voice goes booming along the little town's main street.

And now court has opened. The jury has been sworn in, after much wrangling between lawyers. As every lawyer knows, the selection of the jury is all important and the small town lawyer knows every man in his county, knows his prejudices, what lodge or lodges he belongs to, what church he attends. He has made a hard fight to get on the jury a few men he thinks may be inclined to be friendly to his side of the case.

The lawyers are sitting by a long table before the jury. When there are two lawyers on a side they keep whispering to each other. Witnesses are taken aside for whispered consultations. During the conduct of the case some of the lawyers shout while others speak in low tones. The general opinion is that it is better for the lawyer to do a good deal of shouting. It gives an impression of sincerity, of earnestness, of conviction.

There is a case concerned with a man who has wronged a young girl. She has had a child and the man, who is unmarried, has brought in witnesses to declare that the girl has been the common property of several other men. Her lawyer, as he sums up his case, goes for the young man. He does what Abe Lincoln used to call, "Skinning the witness."

"What kind of a man is it who will get up here in this public place, in this open court, before all these people, and swear away the honor of an innocent young girl, seduced by a soft speaking villain, a man who has made her many promises, has whispered silken lies into her innocent young ears?"

The lawyer takes a handkerchief from his pocket and wipes his eyes.

"Have you men on this jury any young daughters of your own?" he asks.

"I have," he declares. He speaks of two innocent, guiltless young girls in his own house. He shudders. He convicts the man and later the man gets out of it by marrying the girl. He is even a little flattered by the declaration that he, an awkward country boy, is capable of whispering silken words into a girl's ear.

"Oh well," he says, "I guess I'd better marry her, but gee, I made no promises at all."

"I wish I could be dead sure it is my kid," he says.

There is a kind of crude justice to it all, although often witnesses are rather brutally bullied. Many of them, in testifying, keep wandering away from the point.

"Answer yes or no, yes or no," the lawyers keep shouting at them. Efforts are always being made to confuse the witnesses, to catch them making contradictory statements. When several witnesses have agreed before they come to court as to just the story they are to tell, the common mistake is often made of all telling the story too much alike. They agree too minutely in all the details.

"I was coming along the road. It was just ten minutes after nine. I struck a match and looked at my watch."

Other witnesses appear with equally plausible stories as to just how they happened to know the exact time. There is an outbreak of match lighting on a dark country road, all of them suddenly becoming intent on the time. When the witnesses are striving to tell the truth they are uncertain and hesitant. Their stories never exactly agree.

The lawyers jump up and sit down. They hold whispered consultations, make objections to testimony or to the way an opposing lawyer handles a witness. Many of the small town judges are keen-witted men with well developed streaks of humor.

There is a man on trial who has no money to hire a lawyer and the judge appoints two of the town's younger lawyers to defend him.

"I appoint two of you so that each of you will have someone to whisper to," he says.

The people gather into the little small town courtroom. Here is drama straight out of life. Some of the witnesses, country men and women, are so frightened that when they come to the witness stand they speak with difficulty. The judge speaks kindly to them.

"Now don't be afraid. Tell the truth and no one is going to hurt you. I'll look out for you. Face the jury and speak plainly."

There has been a fight between two farm families. The father of a young woman of one family commanded her to have nothing to do with a son of the other.

But the young man has come at night and has parked his car in the road and the young woman has run out to him. One of her brothers saw her go and called his father and the men of her family armed themselves with clubs, stones and pitchforks.

They ran down along a dirt road to the house in which lives the young man's family. He had taken his sweetheart to his own home. They were preparing to go off to town and get married.

A fight started. Stones were thrown and clubs used. The young girl's "men folks" managed to get her away and half drag her along the road to her father's house and the sweetheart has brought the matter into court.

There are frightened confused witnesses. When the young woman is brought to the witness stand she sobs. The father of her sweetheart has long been the enemy of her father. Years before they had a fight over a horse trade. It is a down-to-earth drama, played out in the small town courtroom, witnesses telling lies, witnesses trying to tell the truth. It is living drama of the everyday lives of everyday Americans, played out in the courtroom in an American small town.

## X

Most of the news in the best of the small town weeklies isn't, in the big city newspaper sense, news at all. If there is a revolution in Spain give it a paragraph. If Mr. Morley's little girl gets bitten by a dog and there is danger of rabies, it's worth a column or two. Why not? The whole town is anxious. Nowadays almost every small towner has a radio. He gets the world news and the national news in the same split second as the city man, hears the same wise-cracks, his woman wears the same kind of clothes, hears the same canned music.

The small town newspaper, a weekly, is intensely local. There is column after column of "personals." The idea is to try to catch the color, the smell, the feel of the everyday life of everyday people.

"Mrs. Wilbur of the young married set gave a bridge luncheon on Wednesday."

"Ed Hall's daughter, Julia, has gone to New York, where she has taken a 'lucrative' position."

Julia has an aunt in the city. The aunt is married to a man who works in a gasoline filling station and Julia is really working as a waitress in a small city restaurant but Ed is a regular subscriber to the paper and he has taken out a year's subscription for Julia. You've got to give Julia a break in the news.

It is late fall and the farmers, in the country about town, are killing hogs. It is the time of sausage making, lard making. Very likely the editor will get several good messes of spareribs, brought in by his subscribers. In January Taylor's department store is going to have a big "white sale." Mrs. Kregs slipped on the ice in front of the post office and hurt her hip. It is August and the country is needing rain. The town's water supply is running a little low. One of the town council has been to see the editor. He wants the editor to ask the town people to go a little easy with their lawn sprinkling.

A good editor is a man who runs the little weekly on the theory that his town is the very center of the universe. He knows he can't compete with the big dailies and with the daily radio digests of news. The best of the small town editors are always on the alert for the town news, the little everyday happenings in the lives of everyday people.

**The very center of the universe**

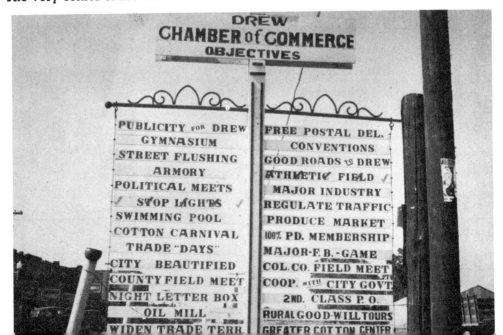

Like the country doctor and the lawyers there is much he knows that he doesn't print. He doesn't intend to get down too deeply under people's skins.

"What's the use?" he asks himself. "If there is a scandal in the town, some married woman getting mixed up with another woman's man, something of that sort, everyone knows it." The editor doesn't aim to rob people of their self-respect. He knows what to print. He knows that life goes hard enough at best with most of his subscribers.

Get their names in the paper is the way to do it, tell as many as possible of the daily happenings in many people's lives. When a citizen of the town dies he gets a good send-off in the paper. On a hook back of his one linotype there are always a number of obituaries, waiting to be dropped into the paper. There is always a literarily-inclined woman in the town who makes a specialty of writing them.

The obituaries tell what church the departed belonged to, it names his relatives. There are usually a few verses touching upon his probable standing "On the Other Shore."

Your Will Smith went from town out to the coal mining country. He was making good out there, saving money. He had got married and had a fine young wife, owned his own home.

"And no sooner did he get all of these fine prospects than ten tons of slate fell on him," the obituary says.

There was a time in the towns, after the 1880's, when the great surge out of the small towns to the cities was at its height, when the American small town weeklies began to go down hill. The earlier weeklies were often mere political organs but among the earlier country editors, all over the country, were many sharp shrewd men. The country weekly produced some of the great writers, the humorists and the wits of their time. There were fighting gun-toting editors, violent men filling their little sheets with violent tirades, editors controlled by state politicians, others because of their wit and humor becoming national figures.

It was a time when the state and national politicians, going from town to town, on speech making tours, could present a new face to every community, a time when few people in the towns took daily newspapers, when there were few telephones. Now the radios in almost every house in town give state, national and world news.

In another day the small town editor, with his little four, six, or eight page paper was the voice of the big outside world coming in. Being a country editor was the first step to political preferment. Country editors became congressmen or U. S. Senators. The editor got railroad passes, could travel up and down his state, go to political conventions. Being a small town editor pretty much meant also being a politician.

And then a change came as changes do come quickly in American life.

The kind of young man, with perhaps a yen for writing, who formerly would have begun his training in the local newspaper office, went off to a nearby city to get a job on a city daily. City firms began to put out what is called "patent insides." For a small sum the editor could get each week whole pages for his paper shipped to him by express, no type to be set, whole pages for his paper all ready to lock into his flat-bed press.

It was pretty vague stuff, most of it, having little to do with the town life. There was a discussion of some national problem, so put that no one reading it could decide whether the writer was for or against the proposition he was discussing, notes on gardening, on women's wear, recipes for cooking. In many towns two-thirds of the local weekly was taken up with matter touching but vaguely the daily lives of the people of the community.

The linotype invaded the country print shop. The journeyman printer, wandering from town to town, always a colorful figure, began to disappear. Men who were mere small town job printers with little or no interest in journalism, were running more and more the country papers, much of the wit and humor of the old time country editor quite gone, the Heywood Brouns, the Frank Adams, the Cappers, the O. O. McIntyres and Peglers who in another age might have stayed in the towns, and become editors of small town weeklies, became city newspaper columnists, writing for syndicates. More and more country weeklies were owned in chains like the grocery stores, the drug stores, and the Five and Tens. Often two-thirds of the space in the town weekly was taken up by material manufactured in Chicago or New York.

Now another change has come. The small town weekly is becoming alive again. There are more and more keen young men coming every year into the field. After the great depression struck America in '29, city streets were filled with good newspaper men out of jobs. The schools of journalism were turning out more young newspaper men. There was a new realization that being a small town editor, with all of its occasional scraping of the pot to get the paper out, the necessity of keeping on the heels of the local merchants for advertising enough to keep going, could mean, after all, a pretty good living.

There is no dead-line for the journalist on the small town weekly. If his paper issues on Wednesday and the fishing is good or it is bird hunting time in the fall the paper can come out on Thursday. The journalist in the small town field doesn't get rich but, if he has at all a flare for it, he can get by, live rather decently. He occupies a position of respect and responsibility in the community. He can stay pretty close to American life as it is lived by the commonalty of Americans, down near the grass roots.

## XI

THE CHURCH BELLS ARE RINGING in the towns, Methodist bells, Catholic, Baptist, Presbyterian, Disciple, Lutheran, Episcopal, Congregational bells. Now the cars are parked thick in all the streets before the churches. Men and women are coming afoot, fathers and mothers, followed by their troops of children. The little girls not minding all the fuss, the hair combing, the scrubbing, the dressing up. It is an instinct.

It begins early in the female. They like it.

See the little boys with their clean shining faces, their carefully combed hair. There goes one who seems to like it. "He is a sissy. That's what he is."

In the towns the Methodists and Baptists lead the procession in the number of churches. North and South, at the time of the last official count, there were some fifty-three thousand white and Negro Baptist churches. The Methodists ran them a close race. The Baptists lead all the others in the number of Negro churches.

Then there are the Roman Catholics with nearly twenty thousand churches, the Presbyterians with about twelve thousand, the Disciples and the Protestant Episcopalians with some seven or eight thousand each, the Church of Christ with six thousand, the Congregational with five thousand, and the Lutherans, counting both the Missouri Synod, the United and the Norwegian Lutheran, with some eleven thousand.

And there are some fifty-five thousand other Protestant churches, the Quakers in many sections strong, the Adventists and the Dunkers, the Christian Scientists, the United Brethren, the Unitarians, the Plymouth Brethren, the Mennonites, not to mention the Great I-Ams, the Zionists, the Two Seeds in the Spirit Baptists, the Christadelphians, the Duck River Baptists, the Shakers, the Holiness churches, the Church of Daniel's Band, the Moravians, and the Defenseless Moravians. The great number and variety of sects, all worshiping the same God is but another expression of American individuality. It is something come down to us out of pioneer days, men and women of many nationalities pouring in, often coming to us to escape religious persecution.

Georgia

South Carolina

New Hampshire

Jim Watson doesn't belong to any church but his wife does, so Jim contributes to the Baptist church in his town. The Baptist preacher meets Jim on the street.

"Jim, now you tell me, why don't you come to church with your wife?"

Jim says he does.

"I come once a year," he says and grins.

"Now you look here, Preacher," says Jim, "I chip in fifty dollars a year, don't I? I come to church once a year. That's fifty dollars a sermon. You haven't got another single member in your church who puts up more than that for just one sermon."

Jim stays at home on Sunday mornings. He reads the Sunday newspaper. It is nice and quiet at home with the wife and kids all gone off to church and Sunday School. Now and then he discusses religion with his special man friend.

"Sure I believe in God," Jim says. "I just think it doesn't make any difference whether a man goes to church or not. I don't think God keeps books on church goers, do you, Ed?"

The old Puritanical tightness of the Sabbath has softened a good deal in the American small town. As everyone knows, it never did clamp down hard on the Catholics.

Formerly, in smaller American towns, there were no Sunday afternoon ball games, on summer Sundays no one but the most pronounced sinners ever went swimming, there were no shows, no movies. But nowadays, in many American towns, the movies are open on Sunday afternoons, there are ball games with teams from neighboring towns, half the town people are out in cars on summer Sunday afternoons, in the churches there is less insistence on hell fires, somewhat fewer revival meetings are held.

The church does however exert a tremendous influence on life in the American small town. Many a Catholic priest, or a Protestant preacher, is first friend to the members of his church when trouble comes.

He is the one who comes in to the family circle when things go bad. He performs the marriage ceremony for the son or daughter. You can talk things over with him. He is taken into the family circle and into the confidence of the family when there is sickness or death. He is there with his hand in that of the husband when a man's wife is on her death-bed, when a son has gone bad, when a daughter has been careless and has got herself into a fix. Often he is able to patch up a break threatened between man and wife, hold a breaking family together.

The church you belong to in the American small town fixes the group you belong to. It fixes your social standing in the town life.

It is the church that takes in the newcomers to the town, his fellow church members seeing that the newcomer meets people, is made to feel a part of the town's life. It is a part of the setup of small town life that enables the young man to meet the girl who will later become his wife.

The church is the center of innumerable activities reaching into many phases of American small town life. It is and remains the channel through which the average American keeps a kind of touch with the mystery, with the strange fact of birth and death, the mystery of stars, of winds, of the renewal of life in nature in the spring.

...San Augustine, Texas

... Cambria, Illinois

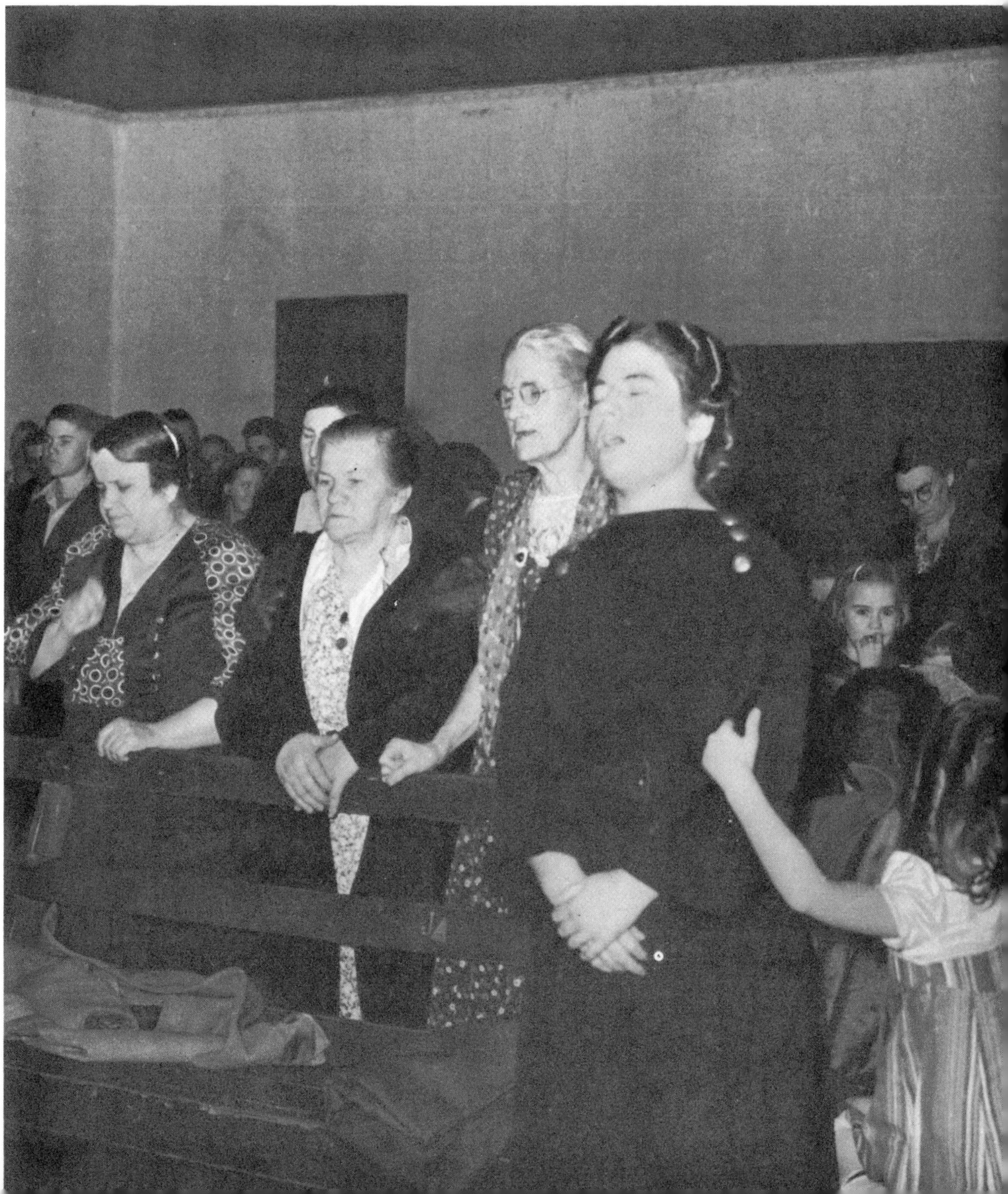

The church you belong to...

...fixes your social standing

## XII

Many American men over forty' love to tell the story of how bravely they stood a beating in school when they were kids and of what little devils they were. It was the thing to do, to put it over on the teacher.

The war between the small town school-teacher and the children in the school went on for a long time. To the average small town child school days were unpleasant and necessary interludes to childhood. There you were, in the schoolroom, on a spring day, and the windows of the room were open. What went on in the room was a dull recital of certain facts. It was impressed upon you that five and five made ten. A certain farmer got into a foolishly complex deal over some apples he had for sale. You had yourself often hung about the cider mill in your town when the farmers were bringing in wagonloads of apples and their business transactions with the cider mill man had never got so foolishly complex. You did a thing called parsing sentences and what an unjust terrible thing to do to a seemingly innocent sentence. You outlined the boundaries of states. It seemed that the state of Arkansas was bounded on the north by Missouri.

Or was it Kansas?

**124**

The school was a kind of prison. How you hated it. What was the good of all this parsing sentences to one who was going to be a railroad engineer, a driver of race horses or to one who, as soon as he got a little older, was going to cut out west and be a cowboy or go off to sea and be a sailor.

There was a man who lived in your town and who was a railroad engineer on the Big Four. You had heard him talk. He was your father's friend and he didn't bother about grammar. You thought that the teacher would have a tough time parsing some of his sentences. You'd be willing to bet anything he didn't know what British general was defeated at the Battle of New Orleans or who won the Battle of Lake Erie. Put it up to him to bound the state of Idaho and he'd be stuck. The Big Four didn't go out there.

The idea of education and its value has always been a passion to the American. The American man is grimly determined that his sons and daughters shall be educated. He wants them to have some chance that did not seem to come his way. The passion is in the poor as well as the rich.

It is in Mrs. Kreiger, whose husband got drunk and was killed by a train. Mrs. Kreiger didn't get much chance when she was a young girl. She had to quit school and go to work in the kitchen of a storekeeper in the town.

Then she got married and her husband wasn't much good and she kept having children.

But Mrs. Kreiger is determined that her children shall have their chance. She dreams of them becoming doctors or lawyers or school-teachers. She will work herself cheerfully into the grave in order that the children rise a little in the world. Sending them to school means that to her.

And gradually, more and more, the school grows closer to the life in the towns. There is a constant increase in the number of American children of the small towns who go out of the grades into the high school. The school building in many towns is nowadays used, more and more, by the whole community. It becomes the town forum, where the problems of the town are discussed. It may be because of the long depression, throwing many of the town's better educated, better prepared, men and women out of other professions but nowadays no one can make a study of our American small town schools without being struck and impressed by the improvement in the quality of the teaching.

In almost every one of our states the school has become the center of the effort to bring education closer to everyday life. There is in many schools more and more intensive study of the individual student, less depends on fixed and rigid tests. In a growing number of schools the problems of citizenship are taken up and studied, the children taught the meaning of such problems as the conservation of soil, the girls taught cooking and dressmaking, the meaning of the courts and of elections brought home to the children, a continual effort to train the hands as well as the head. National questions such as the tariff are taken up and discussed. Often the child of the town schools is taken to the local factory to see goods made, camera clubs are sometimes organized to teach the use of the eye and children are encouraged to make drawings. Local activities of the town are studied, the way the town council works, what becomes of the money collected for the taxes, the setup of the water and sewer systems. All this tends to bring the school closer and closer to the actuality of living in the towns.

## XIII

MANY MEN NOW LIVING CAN REMEMBER the coming of the bicycle, the bicycle followed by the automobile and the coming of hard-surfaced roads, pavement laid down in small town streets and sewer systems installed. The paved roads crept out in all directions, found their way into isolated coal mining towns, into the hill country that in the East and Middlewest separates the North from the South, reached out across the Great Plains, the mountains and the deserts, to the far West.

The man under forty now living in the American small town is living a life that would have seemed as strange as some fictional life on the planet Mars to his father when he was a young man. All the physical aspects of life in the towns have kept changing and changing. Life has taken on a constantly accelerated pace. When the first of the hard-surfaced roads were built, road engineers placed the grades and curves for a car speed of twenty-five or thirty miles an hour. Then cars began to move along the roads, from town to town, past formerly isolated farm houses, at fifty, sixty, and seventy miles an hour.

There was a time, remembered by many older living men, when the American small town had perhaps one telephone, when the receipt of a telegram frightened the citizen to whom it was addressed. Telegrams were sent only in case of death or desperate illness. The old-fashioned, individualistic daily newspaper had disappeared. Newspaper editors like Horace Greeley, James Gordon Bennett, and the later Henry Waterson, men with individual followers in towns all over America, disappeared. The dailies coming to the towns became more and more alike, all served by the same news services. The same newspaper columnists wrote for many newspapers that circulated through the towns, in many towns the same chain store systems, hundreds of thousands, even millions of small town men driving the same make of automobiles.

The Model T's poured out of the great Ford factories. They were in every town, on every country road. The men and boys of the town became Ford-conscious as in our day they are becoming air-conscious.

The great mail order houses came into existence and grew into gigantic institutions, posing a new problem for the town merchants. A hill girl, in a little mountain town of Kentucky, east Tennessee or West Virginia, began to use lipstick, to wear low-priced editions of the latest fashionable city clothes.

The chain stores came to the towns. They were owned outside the towns and in many cases the manager of the store was from the outside. The managers were shifted frequently from town to town. The chain store did little or no banking in the town, the day's receipts being sent away to a central office in a distant city while the man sent in to run the local branch of the chain did not stay long. It was perhaps feared he might make friends, build up a personal following, and then go with a competitive chain or start an independent business of his own.

The old landmarks of the towns, the blacksmith shops, the harness and shoe shops, the livery stable, the carriage builder's shops went rapidly out of business, the livery stable being replaced by the garage and the gas filling station.

Even before the coming of the automobile and the modern development of industry there were sore spots, factory workers sitting in the sun by the factory gate at the noon hour and grumbling about the boss, an occasional badly organized strike. There was the story of the Knights of Labor and the Homestead strike in steel, some of the small town young men, of neighboring Middlewestern states, having joined the local militia, marching off to help put down the strike and coming back to their towns later to tell the story.

In some of the Western mining and lumber towns the I. W. W. fought grimly. They went among the wheat harvesters in the West and the Northwest. In the Pennsylvania, West Virginia, Kentucky, Ohio, and Illinois mining towns, the struggle went on year after year but in the greater number of American small towns the labor struggle was a thing outside the life of the towns, something to be read about in city newspapers. The small towns were marketing centers, shipping points, each with its farm trade territory.

The New England textile industry began to move into the South. There were many reasons for the movement. It brought the industry closer to its source of raw materials.

And there was the vast unused mass of labor, the so-called "poor whites." Theirs was an old and often a desperate story. They were the leftovers of a civilization founded on Negro slavery, the "peculiar" institution of the old South, that, as Abraham Lincoln pointed out, had degraded the idea of labor among the whites. There were these poor whites, often called "trash," even by the slaves, white men who hadn't managed to rise in their world, own land and slaves, nevertheless making up the great majority of the men in the ranks during the long bitter American Civil War.

Reconstruction had done little or nothing for these people and for generations they had been trying to scratch out a living, as tenant farmers, often on worn-out soil. Although they were a miserably poor people and were often illiterate some of them bore names once counted among the big Southern land-owning, slave-owning families.

The poor white family moved eagerly into the mill towns. The mill itself and the company-owned mill town were built outside the corporate limits of an older town. The workers, men and women, and for a long time even the children of eight, ten or twelve, who went to work in the mills, had never heard of labor unions. Vast numbers of them were illiterate.

In the mining towns in many states, labor had long been more conscious. Miners work in small groups in rooms far down underground. Their lives depend upon each other. A kind of brotherhood springs up. The struggle between the miners and the mine owners had gone on year after year, for generations. Often it flared up into open battles, the miners with their guns and the mill guards, employed by the mine company, shooting it out. It was guerilla warfare, sometimes carried on for long months at a time, miners with their rifles lying out on the wooded hills above the mines to pick off the mine guards. Often the state militia was brought in. A Pennsylvania mine owner declared that God had intended certain men to own and profit by the mines. A few great leaders of labor came up out of the ranks of the miners. In certain counties in rich coal mining sections of West Virginia, Kentucky, and Illinois, when a stranger came into one of the little mining towns, he was warned:

"While you are in this town and if you want to keep a whole skin better keep your mouth shut about unions. We don't stand for no union talk here."

There came the crash of '29 followed by the coming of the New Deal. Labor all over America came into a new consciousness.

There was a sudden shifting, a quick change of front. Industry, in the big industrial centers, was suddenly faced with a new labor problem. For the first time in the history of organized labor in America, government began to stand back of labor in its right to organize.

The towns were eager to get new industries. In many towns, in many states, bonuses were offered. The towns raised the money to build factories, they furnished free water, free electricity. Often the industries were offered freedom from town taxes.

The labor struggle became a part of the life of many small towns. In a North Carolina town, where the speed-up had been introduced into a small mill and an efficiency man hired to time the movements of the workers, there was a sudden outbreak. Men and women, made nervous and half hysterical by the presence of the man with the stop watch timing all their movements, suddenly picked up stools and sticks. Women with scissors in their hands and men with their arms full of mill bobbins pursued a frightened efficiency man through the mill yard and through the main street of the town.

In another town the workers, being all deeply religious people, prices of food and clothing having gone up, feeling terribly the need of higher wages, went and knelt before the mill gate to pray.

The little stocking factories, factories making men's shirts and women's garments, came to such a town, stayed as long as they could keep wages down, and then, as the workers became conscious and began to organize, they departed.

The old isolated life of the towns was broken up. The boy or man of the small town, for whose father it had been a great adventure to go for a day to a neighboring town ten miles away, could now cover hundreds of miles in a few hours. He could go into his house and by turning

a knob on a small box could hear the Philadelphia Orchestra playing, hear great singers singing, hear the President or a United States Senator making a speech. Ball games or football games in New York or Los Angeles were described to him play by play.

When the first World War came the younger men rushed to enlist.

The small town boys remembered the romantic stories that had come out of the Civil War, the war that has become to America what the Trojan Wars were to the old Greeks. They went into a new kind of mechanized war, out of which no great heroic individuals could possibly come. It was something new, strange, infinitely horrible. Only the flyers, far up in the air above the battles, could become individual heroes.

And then came the boom days, during and following the war, the famous crash of '29, the experience of prohibition, well-to-do farmers in the farming country for which the town had been the trade center, excited by the high prices of the boom years, going into debt for land at high prices and then going suddenly broke, small towners going into the stock market, many of the so-called middle class of the towns jerked down to a new and lower level of living. Prohibition brought drinking into the homes of the towns as in the cities, the small town barber shop, where formerly only men went, a place of the Police Gazette and shady stories, became a beauty parlor.

At the edge of every town there was a cabaret, a drinking place and dance hall patronized by town and country, some of them innocent enough places, others pretty tough.

Into the towns however as into the cities there has come new frankness concerning all the aspects of life. The mysteries of sex are more openly faced and discussed. In the new generation of youth, growing up in the towns, there is a new boldness, accompanied often by a new fineness, less of an old hypocrisy.

A good deal of the color and the intensity of small town life remains. If there is a wider range of movement, more and more news of the outside world flowing in, there is also a growing disillusionment about leaving the towns for the life of the cities.

For a long time it went on, the continual flow of young life out of the towns to our cities but with the coming of the long depression and the growth of unemployment in the big industrial cities there was a movement back to the towns. The almost universal use of the automobile brought the farmers nearer to town life. Often now the factory hand lives on a farm. If he has no car he pays part of the cost of gas and rides back and forth with a neighbor. Young men and women from the farms go almost nightly into the towns. There are thousands of farm boys over the country who went away to some industrial center but who have now returned.

141

The people dance more. The old bans on card playing and dancing, as evils leading to inevitable ruin, have passed, many of the older people in the towns making a sincere effort to catch up with youth, to understand better the problems of youth in our swiftly changing and perplexing times. With the new opening up of life in the towns, the breaking up of the old isolation, there has been, as in all changes, a gain and a loss. If some of the color has gone, the towns tending to be more and more of one pattern, the terror that was also part of that intensity, the superimposing of moral standards, often almost viciously, the bullying of the young by the old, the Puritanic fear of play, of any expression of joy in life has also, at least partially, been wiped out.

The small towns are and will remain close to the land. Modern machine-driven life has brought the land and the people of the land closer to the towns. There is a growing realization, in the towns, of the meaning of the land, a realization that it is the land out of which has come the vast wealth that has made our America the land of rich possibilities it still remains.

# ABOUT THE PHOTOGRAPHS...

All pictures in this book are a part of the small-town coverage by the Historical Section of the Farm Security Administration. Established under the Resettlement Administration, this photographic project and file is intended to document the living and working conditions of America's rural lower third. Under the direction of Roy E. Stryker a collection of about 35,000 original negatives has been made over a period of five years in all parts of the country. The photographic staff, varying in size according to budget, has never contained more than six photographers at any one moment. These men and women—many of whom are well known in their field—travel on assignment and point their cameras not merely at government projects but at anything in the rural scene which seems significant to them. Nevertheless the FSA file has managed to remain amazingly homogeneous and purposeful. The reason: an inclusive attitude which makes photographer, eye and camera into an instrument of social science.

**143**

The FSA picture record of rural America, still growing daily, has assumed among lovers of photography the integrity of a style. It presents clearly and sharply what has been seen and understood. Impatient with frills and pictorial doo-dads, it has had a sobering and permanent effect on the art of camera in America. With a defined objective always in view, it is helping to outline the necessary cleavage between painting and photography. In the homeland of Hollywood tricks and advertising campaigns, 35,000 bald picture-statements of fact, widely distributed, are doing much to keep photography an honest woman.

The colossal job of recording the ever-changing life of the American land and its people can, of course, never be completed. Already the existing coverage is a magnificent document, varied as weather and topography varies, as crops and yields vary, as men vary, and races of men. In the files are pictures of corn-fields in Iowa that would make a farmer's mouth water, pictures of dust and drought that would dry anybody's throat; bucolic pictures of rural peace, terrible pictures of rural poverty. It can be said without exaggeration that, neatly mounted on gray caption cards in Washington, our time on the land is already becoming history. The most permanent and the most fleeting, the most gay and the most tragic—the cow barn, the migrant's tent, the tractor in the field and the jalopy on the road, the weathered faces of men, the faces of women sagging with household drudgery, the faces of children and the faces of animals; the homely furnishings of a North Carolina farm house, the farmer's overalls, his tools, the share-cropper's rags, and the factory-farm's tractor-fleet—they are all here, photographed in their context, in relation to their environment. In rows of filing cabinets they wait for today's planner and tomorrow's historian.

The Small Town, focal point of rural life, place of exchange, forum of ideas, is a necessary part of such a coverage. For FSA photographers it is a continuous assignment. As they travel from project to project and from state to state, the Small Town is their daily environment: they drive through it, eat in it, sleep in it. Its shooting script is forever in their pockets, calling for pictures of anything from gas stations to town meetings, from cattle auctions to church services. Thus, over a period of years, the FSA Small Town coverage has grown, imperceptibly and almost of itself, into a document of several thousand negatives.

144

Every FSA photographer from the very beginning has had a hand in the telling of the story. Every type of camera from a Leica to an 8 by 10 view camera has been used to picture every type of town—rural town, mining town, company town, cotton town in Mississippi, corn town in Iowa, tourist town in New England. It has been impossible to limit the conception "Small Town" to any definite size. In this book there are pictures from Western outposts with populations of a few hundred, and pictures of small-town aspects of cities with populations in the tens of thousands.

The photographers, some of whose work is here included, are Walker Evans, Dorothea Lange, Russell Lee, Carl Mydans, Marion Post, Arthur Rothstein, Ben Shahn, and John Vachon. The quality of their work is apparent in their pictures. What is not apparent is the exceptionally fine developing and printing, done by those anonymous workers of photography, the laboratory technicians. The FSA laboratory combines factory production with individual craftsmanship.

And, of course, the most important factor in the whole business is the benign influence of Roy Stryker, the man who first conceived the project and now makes it go, the mind that ties the other minds together —which in itself is an achievement of subtle and firm diplomacy. Stryker lives FSA photography. A former cowboy and professor of economics, he takes no pictures. He has enough on his hands what with budgets, appropriations, and the artistic temperament of those who take the pictures for him.

*The Editor.*